15 DAYS OF PRAYER

WITH

Saint Bernadette of Lourdes

FRANÇOIS VAYNE

Translated by Victoria Hébert and Denis Sabourin

Liguori
LIGUORI, MISSOURI

Published by Liguori Publications
Liguori, Missouri
http://www.liguori.org

This book is a translation of *Prier 15 Jours Avec Bernadette*, published
by Nouvelle Cité, 1998, Montrouge, France.

English translation copyright 1999 by Liguori Publications

Library of Congress Cataloging-in-Publication Data

François Vayne
    [Prier 15 jours avec Bernadette. English]
    15 days of prayer with Saint Bernadette of Lourdes / François Vayne ;
translated by Victoria Hébert and Denis Sabourin. — 1st English ed.
      p. cm.
    Includes bibliographical references.
    ISBN 0-7648-0493-6 (pbk.)
    1. Bernadette, Saint, 1844–1879 Prayer-books and devotions—En-
glish. I. Title. II. Title: Fifteen days of prayer with Saint Bernadette of
Lourdes.
BX4700.S65V3813 1999
269'.6—dc21   99–26793

Printed in the United States of America
03 02 01 00 99   5 4 3 2 1
First English Edition 1999

15 Days of Prayer
With Saint Bernadette of Lourdes

Also in this collection:

André Gozier
15 Days of Prayer
With Thomas Merton

André Dupleix
15 Days of Prayer
With Teilhard de Chardin

Michel Lafon
15 Days of Prayer
With Charles de Foucauld

Constant Tonnelier
15 Days of Prayer
With Saint Thérèse of Lisieux

Table of Contents

How to Use This Book

WHEN I THINK BACK TO MY DAYS in the seminary and call to mind those people—professors, spiritual guides, and fellow seminarians—who have influenced me the most in my understanding of the spiritual life, there is one person who immediately comes to mind: Matthew.

Matthew was a soft-spoken young man, new to the seminary, with an understanding of God that went beyond words and completely into action. There were those in my class who weaved a beautiful rhetoric of giving, serving God, and utilizing one's talents for God's greater glory. While these seminarians continued to discuss and debate the act of giving and serving and utilizing, Matthew was outside the seminary, working at a soup kitchen, ministering at an AIDS hospice, teaching someone to read.

As I got to know Matthew better, I soon realized that his soft-spokenness, his quiet demeanor, was not due to excessive shyness or false modesty, but was simply his way of approaching life. It became very clear that Matthew was a man who spoke a language of action and devotion that did not rely on words, a language that provided no space for long-winded theories and discussions about what was the appropriate course of action for a particular situation. Matthew simply acted on the needs he saw around him.

Like Matthew, the saints that impress me the most are those who lived their lives in quiet service to our Lord. Oh, I am impressed and moved by the great speakers, theologians, and Church leaders of our rich tradition, but I am most attracted to those saints who approach God without words, without discussion, in the quiet of their hearts. This is why Saint Bernadette is such a wonderful spiritual guide.

As a young girl, Bernadette Soubirous was a witness to apparitions of Our Lady on eighteen occasions, and was immediately engulfed in a sea of celebrity and controversy. Bernadette never sought such acclaim, consideration, or public interest, and to the best of her efforts attempted to shift all attention given to her to Our Lady and her message of penitence. This escape from attention and celebrity would prove to be a lifelong struggle, however, as even Bernadette's years in the convent were burdened by interviews and examinations concerning what she witnessed at Lourdes during her childhood.

Through it all—the apparitions, the attention, her time in the convent, the illness that confined her to a bed—Bernadette remained humble, saying little, serving God the best she could, and relying totally on divine grace for the strength to face each day with hope and love and patience. This is a simple but extraordinary life, lived totally for God, never seeking glory for its own sake, but always seeking to glorify God.

It is such a joy to be able to spend the next fifteen days in prayer with Bernadette of Lourdes. Surely she welcomes this time as well, ready to pray with us and for us as we deepen our love for God.

Before we actually begin these fifteen days of prayer and reflection, we should keep in mind the importance of time, place, and freedom as regards our prayer life. Prayer is wonderful chance to communicate with God, and it works very well when it is accompanied with some basic structure.

Time: I am not a morning person. Communication with God or anyone else is quite difficult for me in the morning hours. In the evening, however, I am more reflective, more "in tune" with my feelings, and more relaxed. My deepest prayer occurs then, and the time I set aside each night becomes "sacred time," not to be interrupted by anything trivial. Also, this sacred time occurs at nearly the same hour each and every evening. This consistency in dedication to prayer helps to stabilize and fortify my relationship with God. So find that time in the day—be it morning, at break during work or school, before a meal, or in the evening—that suits your prayer life, and devote that time each and every day to the awareness of being in God's presence.

Place: When I was a seminarian there was a spot in our house chapel that I laid claim to and called my own. There, at the end of a pew near the front of the chapel, you could find me on a nightly basis, reflecting on my day, thanking God, and petitioning him for his grace. Place is very important to my prayer life. I need to pray in a place where I am comfortable and relaxed. Now that I am out of the seminary, I pray in a comfortable chair in my bedroom before retiring for the evening. It is a good idea to find your own place of prayer, free from distraction.

Freedom: Yes, freedom! You should feel free in your prayer life; free to be yourself, free to talk to God without holding anything back from his healing love. There is never a need to pretend to be someone you are not when you are in the presence of God. We are all children of the Father, we are all humble creatures of the Creator, and we are all completely loved by God for who we are— right here, right now. There is a joy in feeling free to be who you are, hiding nothing from God, from yourself. Saint Bernadette knew this freedom, the joy it brings, and she wants us to know it, too.

After you set aside a time and a place to freely encounter God during these fifteen days, begin each period of prayer with the most popular (and perhaps most taken for granted) prayer of the Church: the Sign of the Cross. Know that you are with God during this time, and share this special time of prayer to God with Bernadette, reading about her life and reading her words. Let Bernadette take you by the hand, listen to her story, reflect on her words, and pray with her. At the conclusion of each chapter, reflection questions are provided to facilitate further prayer and reflection. Each prayer session can be concluded with a word of thanks to God and the Sign of the Cross.

Bernadette of Lourdes was a woman of few words. Her prayer was intense, though simple, filled with Hail Marys and repeated recitation of such invocations as "Jesus, Mary, and Joseph." Bernadette, it seems, was always ready for God's presence, prepared to meet him in the silence of her heart. Pray that we, too, may open our hearts to God's love and, with Bernadette, know the joy and peace of abiding in his presence.

J.J.C.

A Few Biographical Notes About Bernadette of Lourdes and Nevers

DURING THE FIFTEEN DAYS we are going to live with Bernadette, it would be useful to be able to refer back to the important dates which have been milestones in her life, her "sacred history."

1843: Justin Castérot, a miller, was killed in a cart accident on the road to Poueyferré (France). He had only daughters to run his mill. To remedy the situation and assure continuation of the mill, the family sought a husband for Bernarde, the oldest daughter, and chose François Soubirous, who was a thirty-five-year-old miller. However, he chose her sixteen-year-old sister, Louise, and they married on the 9th of January, 1843. They had nine children, of which only five survived past their childhood: Bernadette (1844); Marie, who was called Toinette, (1846); Jean Marie (1851); Justin (1855); and Pierre (1859)—who was Bernadette's godson.

1844: Bernarde Marie was born at the mill in Boily (France) on Sunday, January 7th—the feast of the Epiphany. On the 9th of January, the wedding anniversary of her parents, she was baptized and her name was changed to Marie Bernarde. Because of her small stature, she was nicknamed Bernadette. In November of that same year, her mother had an accident and severely burned her breast. Since she was expecting another child, she placed Bernadette in the care of Marie Aravant, who lived in Bartrès, a neighboring village. Marie had just lost a baby boy and would wet-nurse Bernadette for the next eighteen months (as was the tradition of the time), because her own mother was unable to do so.

1854: Bernadette was now ten years old. Her quiet family life was upset: her father lost his left eye in a mill accident while "dressing" the millstones, then—as he often gave credit to the poorest of his customers who could not afford to pay him—he, himself, could no longer pay the rent. The Soubirous family was forced to leave "the mill of happiness."

1855: Cholera attacked the small village of a little more than 3000 where the family lived, causing the deaths of about 40 people. Bernadette was affected, but not afflicted, by the disease. This would leave her weak and asthmatic for the rest of her life.

1856: Famine came to Bernadette's region. A poor harvest brought bankruptcy to her father's mill at Arcizac. Her father went to work as a "day laborer," her mother took in laundry (as well as working as a housekeeper and in the fields). Bernadette was put in charge of her siblings. As a result, she was unable to attend either school or Catechism classes. In a census taken on March 7, 1856, the Soubirous family lived on Petits Fossés Street in a squalid hovel.

1857: Bernadette became a cabaret servant at her Aunt Bernarde's inn. The Soubirous family took their four remaining children to live at the "Cachot," a filthy, unhealthy cellar (which was once a jail), loaned to them by their cousin, Sajous. This reduced their living space to an area measuring approximately 12 x 14 feet. On the 27th of March, the police arrested Bernadette's father, accusing him of having stolen two bags of flour from the baker, Maisongrosse. He spent eight days in jail before the charge was dismissed. The complainant stated: "It was their state of extreme poverty that made me believe it could have been him." Bernadette was sent back to the home of her wet-nurse to serve as a babysitter, maid, and shepherdess for pigs and sheep.

1858: On the 20th of January, Bernadette, who felt left out, returned to the "Cachot," because she wanted to learn to read and prepare for her first Communion. She was allowed to attend the free classes given by the Sisters for the poor. She was put in a class with seven and eight year olds.

Early, on the morning of the 11th of February, Bernadette, her sister Toinette, and a friend, Jeanne Abadie (nicknamed Baloume), were out gathering firewood and bones to sell to the local ragpicker in order to be able to buy bread. The first apparition of *Aquero*, "a young woman," appeared— she was dressed all in white, with a blue belt, and a rose at each of her feet. She appeared eighteen times to Bernadette, right up until July 16, 1858, calling for prayers and penitence for sinners. Bernadette made her first Communion on June 3, 1858, during the time of the apparitions.

1860: Bernadette was confirmed on the 5th of February by Msgr. Laurence, bishop of the diocese, who was meeting Bernadette for the first time. On the 15th of July, Bernadette was entrusted to the Sisters of Charity and Christian Instruction of Nevers at Lourdes, classified as a "poor boarder," as a day and boarding student, in an effort to remove her from the public eye.

1862: Official recognition of the apparitions, through a pastoral letter from Msgr. Laurence (bishop of Tarbes), came on the 18th of January.

1866: On the 19th of May, Bernadette attended the inauguration of the Grotto, which was built on the rocks near Massabielle.

On July 3rd, she left Lourdes to become a Sister of Charity (at the motherhouse in Nevers). In religious life, she decided to keep her baptismal name. She became Sister Marie Bernarde on July 29th.

On October 25, 1866, Bernadette made her religious profession, taking her vows in a state of urgency due to her extremely frail health. She was "close to death."

1867: Bernadette renewed her religious vows with forty-five others and received her orders of obedience as a nurse's aide.

1873: Suffering anew, she received the anointing of the sick for the third time, on June 3rd.

1874: At the beginning of January, she became an Assistant Sacristan.

1875: After three occurrences of spitting up blood, which had begun on September 10th, she began her *"work as a sick person."*

1878: Sister Marie Bernard pronounced her perpetual vows on December 9th.

1879: On the 16th of April, Sister Marie Bernard died, at the age of thirty-five, in the infirmary at the Saint Gildard Convent of the Sisters of Charity of Nevers. Her body rests there, incorrupt to this day.

1925: On June 14th, Bernadette Soubirous was beatified by Pope Pius XI.

1933: On December 8th, the feast day of the Immaculate Conception, Bernadette was canonized in Rome.

"The person who exposes himself to the adventure of unconditional love for their neighbor finds God."

Karl Rahner

Introduction

IT WOULD HAVE BEEN EASY to find someone more quali-
fied (than myself) to write this book. The editor insistently
felt that perhaps my pen as a younger journalist could draw
the attention of the readers and focus it, in an original fash-
ion, on a trip to sainthood that we often too quickly believe
we already know. Being a little perplexed at the perspective
of this endeavor, I was fortunate to benefit from the enlight-
ened advice of Father André Doze (chaplain of the interna-
tional Shrine), Father André Cabes (author of a thesis about
the theological meaning of Lourdes), and from a humble religious who did not wish to have her name divulged. I must
sincerely offer my thanks to these three invaluable resource
people. The hospitality of a few days in the shining little community of "Notre Dame de l'Aurore" (Our Lady of the
Dawn)—with an open and prayerful heart—gave me the opportunity to find the necessary serenity to be able to create
this book, even though it was done much too quickly.

I am not going to rewrite the story of the apparitions at
Lourdes. Dom Bernard Billet, Father René Laurentin, and
Father André Ravier have said it all; others could only simply
recopy their work, perhaps, more or less well. I invite you to
consult their books, as well as others on the subject, cited in
the bibliography at the end of this book. What I simply wanted

to do was to take the reader on a prayerful fifteen days with Bernadette, using her actions and words as a basis, trying to keep in mind what she said: *"In trying to dress things up, one only distorts them"* (*Logia* 550 and 576). Here, I bring my five loaves of bread and two fish, like the little boy in the gospel, leaving it up to Jesus to truly feed us.

It is true to say that Bernadette is daunting to me. I had already been devoted to her for eleven years and still, it seems to me, I have everything to discover about her and about "her" Christ. Contrary to the other saints presented in this collection (*15 Days of Prayer With...*), Bernadette did not leave many notes or writings for posterity. *"It is not necessary to write down what I am here to tell you,"* the apparition said with a smile to Bernadette—the one whom she hesitantly named, in the local patois dialect, *"Aquero,"* which means "that one."

Illiterate when heaven opened to her in 1858, the little messenger from Lourdes remained relatively quiet, simply putting the gospel into practice. In this way, she became "the best evidence of the apparition," according to what was said about her by a priest who knew her well. From the photos of Bernadette sent to us, the depth of her expression made an impression on me, and those eyes which saw (the apparition) still strengthen my faith. Her portrait has a place of special importance in my office in Lourdes, like my most precious books.

"Would you do me the honor of coming here for fifteen days?" asked the Lady of the Grotto of a fourteen-year-old pauper girl. Our fifteen chapters could have followed, almost exactly, day by day, the fifteen days of the apparitions and, therefore, confine themselves to the founding event of the greatest pilgrimage in the world. I also chose to bring to light

the prayer that Bernadette said after this time of grace in Lourdes, notably the one during her passion and death—at the age of thirty-five—in the convent of the Sisters of Charity at Nevers. One day, may we all experience what Bernadette attested to in a letter to her mother superior in 1870: *"It is not me who prays, but Jesus in me."*

To Bernadette: *"I don't promise to make you happy in this world, but in the next,"* declared *Aquero*, she who called herself *"The Immaculate Conception."* It is not forbidden, in these words, to see the promise to be able to live a happy life on this earth, not by amassing material goods, but by giving new value to our lives so that, in our own lives, we can see the active presence of the God of Jesus Christ, Bernadette's own God, who infinitely begs for our love.

By writing this book—which I dedicate to all of the "Bernadettes of today"—I saw the abyss of my poverty in all things because I did not know how to pray. I expect that we are all in the same boat, so, let us all put ourselves into the same school as our dear little sister who learned so much from Mary, in particular, the secret of true happiness. When the gospel is really lived, it provides a more complete meaning to the word "conversion"—to turn ourselves toward (the needs of) others, and to break away from "our" narrow world—that is what Gilbert Cesbron summed up in a phrase, attributed to Bernadette, which has spread across the world: "It is enough just to love."

LOURDES, SEPTEMBER 8, 1997,
ON THE SOLEMN FEAST DAY OF THE NATIVITY OF MARY.

15 Days of Prayer
With Saint Bernadette of Lourdes

DAY ONE

A New Sign
of the Cross

There are moments in my life when I am moved to look beyond my fears, beyond my selfish desires, and seek the presence of God around me. I seek out a quiet place, my mind is free from distraction, and I am able to simply listen. And when I listen, I can hear the words of God, and discern his will; I can hear the saints, and hope in their intercession; I can hear the Blessed Virgin Mary, and take comfort in her assurance that answering yes to God is saying yes to life, to love, and to salvation.

"The Blessed Virgin chose me
because I was the most innocent thing
in the world's eyes."

G od always chooses hearts that are empty enough to welcome his grace. He looks for arms that are open to the
gifts he wants to give. The first apparition to Bernadette by
"the young lady" contained, in a mysterious way, the call for
us to free ourselves so we can learn to pray, so that we can
align our desire to receive with God's own desire to give.

On the morning of the 11th of February, 1858, Bernadette
went to the grotto at Massabielle, which was a rocky cliff
where the waterway deposited dead wood and rock chips;
"there, where the mill canal rejoins the River Gave," in the
place where the municipal pork farmer, Samson, normally
herded his pigs. With her sister, Toinette, and her friend, Jeanne
Abadie, Bernadette went to gather dead wood to sell to the
ragpicker so she could buy bread.

"The first time I went to the Grotto was on Thursday, February 11, 1858. I went to gather dead wood
with two others *(Toinette, her sister, and Jeanne
Abadie, her friend)*. When we arrived at the mill (of
Savy), I asked the two others if they wanted to go see
where the water from the mill went to join the River
Gave. They said yes. From there, we followed the canal. Once we got there *(at the foot of the Massabielle
rock)* we found ourselves in front of a grotto. Since
we could go no further, my two companions began to
cross the water which was in front of the grotto; therefore, I found myself alone on the other side. They
crossed the water and began to cry. I asked them why
they were crying. They replied that the water was cold.
I asked them to help me throw a few rocks into the
water so I could cross it without removing my shoes.
They told me, in so many words, to do what they had

done. Then I went along a little further to see if I could cross without taking my shoes off, but that was impossible. I came back to the front of the grotto and started to take my shoes off. As soon as I had removed the first sock, I heard a noise that sounded like a gust of wind. Then I turned my head toward the fields. I saw that the trees were very calm and continued to remove my shoes. I again heard the same noise. As I lifted my head, looking towards the grotto, I saw a woman dressed all in white, in a white dress with a blue belt, and a golden rose (the same color as her rosary) on each foot; the beads on her rosary were white. The Lady made a gesture with her finger for me to approach her, but I was seized with fear. I did not dare. Believing that I was faced with an illusion, I rubbed my eyes, but that was in vain. I looked again and I still saw the same Lady."

At this point in Bernadette's story, it is the image of the bare feet of the Lady that strikes me and brings to mind the words of the prophet Isaiah (52:7): "How beautiful on the mountains are the feet of the messenger who announces peace...." This is a message of inner peace that will be given to us.

Bernadette continued her story:

"Then, I put my hand into my pocket and took my rosary. I wanted to make the Sign of the Cross, but it was in vain: I could not raise my hand up to my forehead, it collapsed on me. Then shock got the better of me; however, I didn't leave. The Lady prayed the rosary she held in her hands and made the Sign of the

Cross. Then I stopped being afraid. I again took up my rosary and managed to make the Sign of the Cross. From that moment on I felt perfectly calm. I knelt down and said the rosary, all the time having this Lady right in front of my eyes. The vision fingered the beads of her own rosary, but she didn't move her lips. When I finished my rosary, the Lady made a sign for me to approach, but I didn't dare. I always stayed in the same place. Then, all of a sudden, she disappeared. I started to remove the other sock to cross the little bit of water which was in front of the grotto, so that I could join my companions. And then we went away. Along our way back home, I asked my companions if they had seen anything. They both answered 'no' but asked me 'did you see something?'—I answered: 'Oh no, if you didn't see anything, neither did I.' I thought that I had been mistaken. But, while we were walking back, all along the road, they kept asking me what I had seen. I didn't want to tell them. Seeing that they were constantly coming back to the subject, I decided to tell them, but on the condition that they tell no one. They promised to keep the secret. They told me that I should never return there, and neither should they, believing that it was someone who wanted to hurt us. I said I didn't think so. As soon as we arrived home, they hurried to tell that I had seen a Lady dressed in white. This is the story of the first time...."

From the time of the first meeting, *Aquero* seemed to want to rob Bernadette a little of what she thought she knew: her Sign of the Cross! She couldn't even manage to do it. Her hand fell to her side like it was paralyzed and "shock got the better of her."

However, Bernadette, your deprivation had already been extreme. Your parents had been stranded at the "Cachot" because they had failed in their attempt to keep the mill going. They lived miserably, having nothing except God, "crying out in prayer" every evening, as their cousin Sajous related. It was because the family had no more wood that your mother, Louise, took the chance and sent you to look for some, at the risk of provoking an asthma attack. You went to the grotto because, at least there, no one would think you were a thief. The daughter of a prisoner, you were haunted by the unjust arrest, the year before, of François, your father, who was wrongly accused of having stolen two bags of flour. You returned to Lourdes, from Bartrès, just a few days before the first apparition, because you absolutely wanted to begin school. At the age of fourteen, you knew nothing and you must think about making your first Communion. And then *poof!*, this *"young lady,"* as young and small as you, appeared from the crevices in the rock, after you heard a noise, *"like there had been a gust of wind...."*

We will probably never have the opportunity to live such an experience as this one, but we can receive, with you, Bernadette, a new Sign of the Cross. It was so beautiful, so broad and penetrating, that it would be your first silent sermon, changing the hearts of those who would see it—Duffo the chairmaker, or Father Sempé....

Beyond these stories, it is, above all, these three steps of initiation, undertaken by Mary with Bernadette, which interest me about this first day. I renounce what is old, to "the former man," who thought, from within, that he knew and believed. I enter into a new world of faith. I receive, into my body, this newness that comes from God. And I take the time to trace the Sign of the Cross like I had never before been given the power to do. I go from the head to the heart, as if I am going to the wellspring of love. I cross this vast distance—sixteen inches—which will change my attitude toward God and others.... "If you want to know Christ, never look for him without the cross" (Saint John of the Cross).

The cross, the sign of love, is, at the same time, both a call and a commitment to take what is real onto our shoulders, to bear the weight of reality in full confidence that we are doing our work in harmony with the Holy Spirit, who handles what we can't do alone....

Lord, you open my eyes to the signs of your presence which make the story of Bernadette a saintly story. It is also my own story, if I really realize the marvels you have made in my life. Yes, in Lourdes, we are thrown into a biblical atmosphere: a gap has opened in us to let the light of love, which comes from the cross, enter. This sign—taken from the ancient alphabet—evoked in the book of Ezekiel (9:3–6), marks the foreheads of those who cry and wail over all the abominations committed in Jerusalem.

Seeing Bernadette, stopped by the frigid water at the edge of the canal which seemed to be impassable, reminds us vividly of the people led by Moses and blocked by the Red Sea, before the dry crossing and destruction of Pharaoh's armies....

Bernadette, who took her shoes off, awakens us to the memory of Moses who was invited to remove his shoes in order to approach the burning bush (Ex 3:5): "Remove the sandals from your feet, for the place on which you are standing is holy ground."

With regards to this "rumor," does it not announce a presence like the sound of the Lord God walking in the garden at the time of the evening breeze (Gen 3:8)? I think back to Elijah, at Mount Horeb, who recognized your presence, Lord, in a light breeze, who saw you "at the entrance of the grotto" (1 Kings 19:13). The Acts of the Apostles also teaches us that the coming of the Holy Spirit will be accompanied by "a gust of wind" (Acts 2:2).

Through the light of your words, Lord, I understand, above all, that Bernadette had been chosen for a mission of salvation because she was the smallest of the small, like the little David had been called by the prophet Samuel (1 Sam 16:7). You want to make us kings and queens. Lord, if only we would agree to abandon our certainties and intellectual or material security!

At least I am rich in ideas, a little weighted down by my talents and my goods, and above all, my will....

To live to the depth of the grand adventure of faith, it is necessary for us to see ourselves as poor, recognize ourselves as vulnerable, let ourselves love. "God chose what is foolish in the world to shame the wise; God chose what is weak in the world to shame the strong" (1 Cor 1:27). I have noticed that when we ask something from someone we feel insignificant; God lets unrecognized powers of love awaken in us and those we ask. And what would happen if we had more confidence in the poverty that waits inside of ourselves? It is through accepting our smallness, our consentual infirmity, that the grace of God works with the most strength: "Lower yourself then, make yourself small, and you will grasp (Christ)," wrote Saint Bernard of Clairvaux, Doctor of the Church and patron saint of our Bernadette.

REFLECTION QUESTIONS

The Lord our God, the holy saints, our Blessed Mother—
they are always with me; guiding, hoping, assuring. Can I
turn my eyes from myself and gaze upon them there, beside
me? Do I see them there? Do I recognize their love for me?
And do I listen when they speak to me?

DAY TWO

Happiness Promised, Today

FOCUS POINT

One of the criminals who were hanged there kept deriding him and saying, "Are you not the Messiah? Save yourself and us!" But the other rebuked him, saying, "Do you not fear God, since you are under the same sentence of condemnation? And we indeed have been condemned justly, for we are getting what we deserve for our deeds, but this man has done nothing wrong." Then he said, "Jesus, remember me when you come into your kingdom." He replied, "Truly I tell you, today you will be with me in Paradise" (Lk 23:39–43).

"I don't promise to make you happy
in this world, but in the next."

In order to explain what she saw, Bernadette used the language of mystery in much the same way as Saint Luke did his gospel stories about the childhood of Christ. She called the vision *"Aquero,"* a "patois" word (local dialect) which means either "that one" or "that thing there"—"Something" in white. The shepherds, alerted by the angels, went to Bethlehem to see "who" had come. They related "what" had been told to them. "These things." And "that" also happened in a grotto, a place of new birth, for us, as for millions of other pilgrims, for almost a century and a half.

At the time of the second apparition, February 14th, Bernadette entered into a profound state of ecstacy. They thought she was dead. Louise Soubirous renewed her ban on going to the grotto.

"The second time was the following Sunday. I went back there because I felt forced to, from inside of myself. My mother had forbidden me to go there. After High Mass, the two others and I went back to again ask my mother. She didn't want me to go, she told me that she was afraid I would fall into the water and that I wouldn't be able to come back to help with vespers. I promised her that I would. Then, she gave me permission to go. I went to the parish church to get a bottle of holy water to sprinkle on the vision when I was at the grotto if I saw it. Once there, each of us took our rosary and knelt to recite it. As soon as I had said the first decade, I noticed the same Lady. Then I went to sprinkle the holy water, telling her that if she had come on behalf of God to stay and, if not, to leave. She smiled and bent down. The more I sprinkled her, the more she smiled and bent her head and the more I saw her making signs. And then, seized with fear, I hurried to sprinkle her until the bottle was empty. Then, I continued to recite my rosary. She disappeared and we returned to go to vespers. That was the second time." *Mary had prepared the young visionary for the great moment of her first words.*

On the 18th of February, Bernadette went to the grotto, thanks to the intervention of Madame Milhet, Louise Soubirous' employer, who wanted to see what was happening.

"The third time, the following Thursday, I went to the grotto with some important people who suggested that I take pen and paper along and ask her that if she had anything to tell me to be so kind as to write it down. I said these same words to the Lady. She smiled and told me that it wasn't necessary to write down what she had to tell me. She then asked me if I had the graciousness to come back here for fifteen days. I replied yes. She also told me that she didn't promise to make me happy in this world, but in the next."

"It is not necessary to write down what I have to say to you," replied the "little young lady." She gently, but firmly, pushed the inkstand aside. The divine approach always demands a renunciation, a purification. And the new covenant must etch itself into the depths of my heart, not on stone or paper.

Bernadette, you heard *Aquero* say *"you"* and then ask you to be so gracious as to return for fifteen days. She spoke to you in your own patois dialect, with respect and honor for you, the daughter of an unemployed father and a housekeeper. She saw you *"as a person."* Didn't you say that this special attention upset you? I am reminded of the Samaritan woman at the well who was surprised that Jesus, a Jew, asked her to give him something to drink (Jn 4:9)....Lourdes is the reversal of values, the gospel which comes out of the Sunday homilies to be lived through concrete acts in our lives.

Then comes the great phrase which would control the entire message of the apparitions. We believe that Mary promised Bernadette the "happiness of heaven." One day, she made a comment about this phrase: *"The Blessed Virgin did not lie to me: the first part of her words can be confirmed; that, I hold firm to, I am sure I have it"* (*Logia* 790). What has struck your contemporaries is your mysterious joy, Bernadette. You find yourself *"happier than a queen on her throne."* From this life onward you will become secretly introduced into *"the next world,"* more and more.

Isn't prayer a personal meeting with the Lord? He promises: "Those who love me...my Father will love them and we will come to them and make our home with them" (Jn 14:23). The happiness of the next world, I feel it from here on earth. It is my faith, like Bernadette and many others. Lord, you want to extricate me from my own "little world"—and from this "me" to which I am stuck—you want to open me to my neighbor's world, to his suffering, his truth. I can only be happy in this movement by which you set me apart from others. *"I don't promise to make you happy in this world, but in the next."* It is there that we find the reality of a Christian vocation, where suffering is present to the very end. "You, yourself, even a sword will pierce your soul," predicted Simon to the Blessed Virgin who presented her child to the Temple. In my daily life, what meaning can I give to such suffering? Is it that I see the workings of the strength of a new life there, like a flower stem which rips the dry ground apart to make way for the growth of beauty and new life? The happiness of the next world already pierces through, under the appearance of our daily trivialities—and that hurts, at times, quite often, but God continuously gives me new life through these pains.

Today, my prayer is to trust. *"I felt that the Good Lord wanted it. When we think that the Good Lord permits it, we do not complain."* These words, from Bernadette's soul, with reference to the misfortunes that befell her family before the apparitions, invite me to this trust, the highest principle of faith. Lord, I want to receive, little by little, the innocence and simplicity of Bernadette....

Jesus, today and each moment from now on, lead me on the road of transparency.... I want to see you, I want to love you in each person I meet. The next world is now when I love in this manner, when I love you!

Bernadette felt *"forced from inside of herself"* to go to the grotto. Do I feel forced to listen to God who speaks to me through the people I meet? Do I consider it important to discover what he wants to tell me in each circumstance? Every day, this divine presence makes itself felt, but I am deaf, blind, too distracted by other projects, or dependent upon reasonable recommendations by my advisors. Lord, make me a free being, connected to your calls, able to immediately reply to the whim of your meetings because you want my happiness.

I feel forced from inside of myself, like you, Bernadette, because a great love is waiting for me. No one can tear this conviction away from me and I will go towards the light, united to my Lord. He will help me master the ability not to judge based on false values, and to remain free with respect to all fads, by accepting to be poor and "foolish" to the eyes of the world.... Jesus waits for me, here and now, to live in the Holy Spirit.

REFLECTION QUESTIONS

Do I feel "forced from inside myself" to move toward you, O Lord Jesus? Am I moved by my love for you to do your will and experience the joy of living my life to glorify you, O Lord? Do I seek the happiness there is to be found in loving you, God, the happiness in loving you in this world that leads to eternal happiness in the next?

DAY THREE

When God Hides, He Does It to Better Give of Himself

FOCUS POINT

In the lives of even the greatest saints there are periods of spiritual dryness, times when God seems to be absent. This desert without an oasis can be disconcerting—that is, until I look very closely. Because, even in the desert, there are signs of life. There are plants growing from the crevices of rock, nourished by a wellspring deep below the dry and dusty surface. In these times of spiritual dryness I can seek this wellspring, I can discover new depths of joy and peace in my relationship with Jesus.

"How did I fail her?"

Historians have difficulty reconstituting the events which occur on different days. For Bernadette, the *"fifteen days"* were the time when the Lady confided her messages and secrets to the peasant girl. The calendar meant little to Bernadette; she had no memory except for that which concerned the absence of the vision.

"I returned there for fifteen days. The vision appeared every day with the exception of a Monday and a Friday. Many times she repeated to me that I should tell the priests that a chapel must be built there and to go to the fountain to wash myself and that I must pray for sinners. In the space of fifteen days, she gave me three secrets which she prohibited me from telling to anyone. I have been faithful up until now."

The radiance of Bernadette during the apparitions attracted many people. The atmosphere of prayer and peace which emanates from Massabielle—literally the "old rock"—is extraordinary. Is it not an analogical matter that "this rock that the builders rejected has become the chief cornerstone" for a new spiritual temple? (Ps 118:22 and 1 Pet 2:7). This will all be revealed, little by little.

On the 20th of February, there were about thirty people there. The police were concerned and intervened by approaching François Soubirous, who promised that he would ban Bernadette from returning to the grotto—but he knew his eldest daughter better than that....

Bernadette was interrogated by the police commissioner, but since her family was afraid, she obeyed and went to school on the 22nd of February. In the afternoon, an invincible force drew her to Massabielle. Her mother said: "The little one is not a liar. She is not disobedient but she said that she was forced to go there by something that she cannot explain." But on this particular afternoon *Aquero* wasn't there....

Bernadette, the day without seeing the apparition left traces of uncertainty on your face: *"I don't know how I failed this Lady."* She asked herself: *"What did I do to her? Is she angry?"* In the evening, she went to Father Pomain, the parish vicar, for confession. He concluded: "They have no right to stop you from going." Those events do not fall under the jurisdiction of the law....

Again, on the 26th of February, the apparition did not appear. François Soubirous withdrew his ban and Louise, the mother, continued to fear imprisonment. These contradictions were serious and disturbed Bernadette. She would be very affected by the absences of the Lady on the Monday and Friday.

With hindsight, we are able to see, in this trial, a necessary stage in all prayer life. The Lord doesn't always appear when we await him. Let us think of the great dry spells that Thérèse of the Child Jesus experienced in her life at Carmel, especially in the last year of her life. Christ is, nevertheless, closer to us than ever in these moments of seeming absence. How many times have these "absences" discouraged us? When these times occur again, let us remind ourselves of Bernadette's spiritual experience, so that we may persevere. These empty days, when God hides himself, are important because they give us the opportunity to show our faithfulness and show that our love is given freely.

A trial of faith purifies me and makes me grow. To those who are favored with visions or other supernatural phenomena, the great mystical authors make the recommendation to control what happens and even resist them. And then, today, if I am tempted to doubt Bernadette's story, don't these absences, by the Lady, tend to prove the truthfulness of her claims? If Bernadette was playing a joke, why didn't she play it out on the Monday and Friday? Therefore, something did happen when she said that she saw....All realities, negative or lived as such, could be the beginning of a greater spiritual gift.

Jesus, I heard you cry out on the cross: "My God, my God, why have you forsaken me?" (Ps 22:1 and Mt 27:46). You didn't even have enough strength to call the one you were addressing "Father," but this cry reached deeply into the heart of all my solitudes. I am no longer alone. No situation, no matter how dramatic, can separate me from you, since, in my darkness, it is you who cry out and, united with you, I will find my way back to the road of life. I will travel the dark tunnels with the assurance that day will come again. My God, of whom I am sure, you are closer to me than I could ever imagine! Your presence is real, beyond all feelings, all words, all images. Your presence dwells in me and sustains me without me even knowing it. For me, to live is to live in you. And, in the void of your silence, my soul rests in peace, it blossoms according to the amount of love with which you have filled it.

With you, Lord, like Bernadette, I will make the passage from appearance to transparency in order to become what I say about you. "Because Bernadette never reflected about herself, she reflected—that is to say, let pass through herself, without tarnishing, like plate glass—the light which has been shone on her" (Hans Urs von Balthasar). Faith goes beyond our sensory experience. It is the personal gift of a God who offers himself and has nothing in common with paranormal or esoteric communication....

Mary's absence on the Monday and Friday of the fifteen days of apparitions brings us to simply conclude that we must not confuse Revelation with revelations.

Bernadette made her first Communion on June 3rd, the feast day of the Body of Christ (Corpus Christi). She traveled from Bartrès to Lourdes for this: *"It was necessary for me to return home: the Parish Priest is going to prepare the children for their first Communion, and if I go to Lourdes, I will make it there."* *Aquero* came to teach her and teach us to become a dwelling for God, to dwell in him—a greater marvel than all the visions, conversations, and "messages...."

The tabernacle, installed at the back of the grotto at Lourdes, gives meaning to the days without apparitions. Let us go, on a regular basis, to turn our thoughts to God before the tabernacle, the one in the closest church. And, in the absence of all "apparitions," let us make a new act of faith. It is not in a hurricane, an earthquake, or a fire that God will come to me (1 Kings 19).... He made himself a small child in Bethlehem two thousand years ago, and today he gives himself to me, in the form of bread and wine, always defenseless, always into my hands, delivered and abandoned. His silence allows me the freedom to love him, freely. At a time when many turn the tables to speak of "spirits," and amuse themselves by having close contact with the "dead," Bernadette invites me to another spiritual connection, one even more straightforward, more true and so much more fruitful. Love never imposes itself, it does not make one afraid. Love is revealed in a game of hide and seek which helps me simply live the ordinary in an extraordinary way...with the risen Jesus in the glory of his Father on the great morning when the tomb was empty.

Absence and want open a space for an endless communion, which is even deeper than before, and steadfastly reveals the quality of a presence. "When I close my eyes, I see you." Who has not experienced this heartfelt memory where there is an indelibly etched face?

REFLECTION QUESTIONS

Am I disconcerted when my prayer-life encounters a period of dryness, a feeling that God is far away? Or do I find that these times afford a wonderful opportunity to discover God in those places, and in those people, where I would not usually look? Do I seek to find God in all things, and experience communion with him at those times when his presence is not obvious to my limited sight?

DAY FOUR

A Change of Heart

FOCUS POINT

When I turn my attention to God and face him, I turn my attention away from those things now behind me—things that are not God, things that restrict me and bind me, keeping me from giving everything that I am to him who deserves all my love. When I turn like this I am penintent, turning from the old, "dead" way of life, to the new, life-giving existence that comes only from God.

"Penitence, penitence, penitence..."

W e are now in the midst of the apparitions. On the 19th of February, there are only eight people present; thirty on the 20th and more than a hundred on the 21st. On the 23rd, there is a crowd. Some notable people have come with the intention of mocking the popular naiveness. On the

24th, Mary began her great requests with reference to sinners. Lent had begun on the 17th.... A week later, on Thursday, the 25th, *Aquero* pronounced the word *"penitence"* three times. Bernadette reflects the profound sadness of the Lady when she evokes the word *"sinners."* The second phrase: *"Pray for the sinners,"* gives the true meaning to the word *"penitence."* This word was a part of the Church vocabulary of the time. They spoke of the sacrament of penitence, from Latin, which itself was a translation from Greek for a biblical word that meant "a change of heart."

Mary came to invite me to conversion, to a change of heart. She takes up where Jesus left off: "The time is fulfilled, and the kingdom of God has come near; repent, and believe in the good news" (Mk 1:15). Lourdes, the land of the gospel! Bernadette obeyed the requests for penitential acts which were given in an astonishing manner on the 24th of February. Is not the profound meaning of all true prayer a passage from the natural man—physical, animal—to the spiritual man? (1 Cor 2:14).

I can't put off this change of heart until later. It is a continuous action, like an athlete who is always training. Afterwards will be too late. Truly, it is already long overdue. Often, I have retreated when faced with an obstacle. Here and now, my own outlook must change. Do I accept myself just as I am, do I love the suffering Christ enough within myself? Do I enter, with the others, into God's longstanding patient benevolence? Do I look at them with a hopefulness that grows, or, to the contrary, with a judgmental look that paralyzes and destroys? Am I an accomplice to widespread slander? Penitence is not so much deprivation, as it is a movement of love which is always renewing itself—do I know this? I am not a champion of prayer or adoration, but it is within my grasp to love. To love, because "God is Love," as Saint John, the apostle, wrote: "…and those who abide in love, abide in God and God abides in them" (1 Jn 4:16).

Bernadette, your calm happiness affected the excise-tax officer, Estrade, who came "to see what was happening" on February 23rd. At the grotto, they said it was "a Lenten carnival, without the permission of the parish priest." Estrade became a believer and a witness. The man who had snickered was converted, he had a change of heart. At the Café Français, where one could find members of Lourdes' middle class, he stood up to all those self-important people and shook their hypocritical strongholds.

The beauty of Bernadette in her ecstacy, "more beautiful than that of Rachel, the celebrated actress of the time, at the very height of her career," was marred by a veil of sadness on Wednesday, the 24th. *"Pray to God for the conversion of sinners,"* said the young lady of the rock, who was as young and of the same petite stature as Bernadette, who herself stood only four foot eight inches tall (4'8"). *"Aquero was sad,"* said Bernadette. The Lady requested that the child prostrate herself while kissing the ground (in penance) *"for sinners."* This gesture reminds me of a similar one done by Pope John Paul II when he is traveling. It is a gesture of solidarity, of profound fraternity, and of great humility. Mary also came down, through the inner fissure of the rock vault in the grotto, so that she could get closer to Bernadette, just as God came close to her in Nazareth.

To be a Christian is to live this closeness to the questions of humanity, to its sorrows and its hopes. It is not to retreat to an eagle's nest with those who believe themselves to be pure and just.

Bernadette, you discovered, through the sadness of a

glance, this thought about sinners, which would remain with you for the rest of your life. In 1872, you wrote to Mother Alexandrine Roques: *"Let us pray a great deal for these poor sinners. After all, they are our brothers."* Our brothers? Me, your brother? How can I be your brother when I am so far from this ideal to which I aspire? And those I meet—who seem to me to be even farther away than I am from this ideal—they are my brothers? A brother to love, to understand, and to help when he stumbles. For that person, like you, I am called to put the request of the Virgin into practice: *"Penitence."*

The gospel, once again, reveals its timelessness: "In those days John the Baptist appeared in the wilderness of Judea, proclaiming, 'Repent, for the kingdom of heaven has come near'...and they were baptized by him in the river Jordan, confessing their sins" (Mt 3:1–6). But, we can't buy ourselves a good conscience at a bargain price to reassure ourselves: "Bear fruit worthy of repentance.... Even now the ax is lying at the root of the trees; every tree therefore that does not bear good fruit is cut down and thrown into the fire," as John the Baptist told us (Mt 3:8–10).

All-powerful Lord, remove the affectations from me that make my prayers a ridiculous drama. Like the fourth stained-glass window in the Major Basilica in Lourdes, which shows the eighth apparition, make me see the Lamb of God resting on the sacred book with the seven markers that remind us of the seven sacraments, the seven sources of my hope. Am I ready to give my life, from one moment to the next, so that the fire of the gospel sets the entire earth ablaze? We don't light a blazing fire with a big log, but with kindling; I must love the little things....

The major contribution of the congregation to which

Bernadette will commit herself—we will see this later—after a long period of reflection, will be to help everyone to recenter themselves explicitly on love which we then will call by the word "charity," henceforth very besmirched. The founder of Bernadette's future religious family had already captured the central aspect of love: "Your major duty is the one that Jesus Christ recommended to you: that is to say, charity. All you need in order to fulfill your duty perfectly is to be charitable, since anyone who is charitable fulfills God's law, according to the teachings of Saint Paul" (Rom 13:8–10 and Gal 5:14).

Bernadette's entire life translates, through its ups and downs, this requirement to love. "I have never heard anything come out of her mouth that was against anyone," said one of her religious sisters. Even her comments, which were often sharp, were "never hurtful." My own conversion begins there....

If, in its first movement, the Sign of the Cross makes my hand go from my idea and my will to my heart, where God abides, the second movement of this "sign" makes me bring the extremes together, to reconcile the conflicts—as I bring my hand, which comes from the heart, from the left shoulder to the right—to channel the strength of love into service for unity. "Love each other." "So that all will be united so that the world believes." That is the key of true penitence, in order to achieve your "will," Jesus, your most cherished desire. "That they all may be one" (Jn 17:21), like the Father and you are One in love....

REFLECTION QUESTIONS

Do I seek to recenter myself in God through penitence? Am I open and trusting enough of God to bring to him those dark and shameful parts of my self that only he can heal, that only he can make clean, that only he can look beyond, seeing the humble creature he knew and loved before he formed me in the womb?

DAY FIVE

To the Springs of Baptism

FOCUS POINT

"I baptize you with water; but one who is more powerful than I is coming; I am not worthy to untie the thong of his sandals. He will baptize you with the Holy Spirit and fire" (Lk 3:16).

"Go drink at the spring and wash yourself there."

Lord, you know my sin, my egoism, my pride, which drive me to be critical of others and you know all of my hidden distress. Bernadette imitated your passion for me on the 25th of February, 1858. She told me how to recognize you immediately there, where I believe you are not present, and especially during the night of my treason, my laziness, and my calculated omissions.

"The Lady told me that I must go to the fountain and wash myself there. Not seeing what she meant, I went to drink at the Gave (River). She told me that it wasn't there; she made a sign with her finger for me to go under the rock. I went there; and there, I found a little water which looked muddy, in such a small quantity that I could only take a little in the hollow of my hand. Still, I obeyed and I began to dig deeper; afterwards, I could take some. It was so dirty that I threw it away three times, but on the fourth attempt, I could drink some. She also made me eat a certain herb which is found at that same place where I drank, only once, it doesn't matter why. Then, following that, the vision disappeared and I stepped back."

T he spring predated the apparitions, but was lost in the enormous layer of moraine (rocky debris). From humid and muddy soil a surface trickle could, at times, flow out at a point on the slope but not flow on the surface itself to the Gave. Therefore, it was not *Aquero* who made this water spring forth. She only enhanced its value so that we would go there to drink. But for what reason? Let us try to understand it.

The apparition of the 25th of February was truly the heart of all apparitions: it was the seventh of the thirteen that occurred during the fifteen days—six before and six after—as if the Lord wanted to underline its central aspect. Bernadette covered herself with mud and made herself look silly to the eyes of those who had admired her the night before. She resembled Christ during his passion, a striking parallel to the Church liturgy which was made to be read that day, from the

Gospel of Saint John (19:34): "One of the soldiers pierced his side with a spear, and at once blood and water came out." The spring is the mystical sign of this water which ran with the blood from Christ's side, pierced by the soldier's spear. The true pilgrimage begins: those who follow from now on will go beyond simple curiosity. Bernadette shares the immense sadness of the Lady regarding sin: "We could have said that she bore all the sorrows of the world," stated a witness, Marie Pailhès.

The spring began to flow, muddy and repulsive at first, then clear and beautiful. "Jesus spat on the ground, made mud with his saliva and spread the mud on the blind man's eyes saying: 'Go wash in the pool of Siloam' (which means Sent). Then he went and washed and came back able to see" (Jn 9:6–7). Mud is, without a doubt, the sign of a new creation.

This water will permit the Lord to heal physical ailments, but above all, makes reference to baptism, which heals sin, the ultimate ailment. We are all ailing, sometimes without even knowing it, and one day, we will go there with a great desire to bathe and relive our baptism: 400,000 people bathe themselves in the Lourdes springs annually.... Lourdes, like a gushing spring at the crossroads of seven valleys, come and refresh the old Rome of seven hills—the Church which bends under two thousand years of glory and sad history—bring it freedom and simplicity, the philter (love potion) of eternal youth, and the secret of joyous radiance of those who march towards a new Jerusalem....

The ninth apparition pushes us to discover our mud, our sin, and have the will to turn to God in order to receive the water which purifies and quenches, the water of our baptism, which has perhaps stagnated for a long time under piles of lies and falsehoods.

Bernadette, it is you who appears to me, the unrecogniz-able face, smeared with mud. You are chewing the herbs picked from the muddy soil, reminding us that man too often deifies the "ox that eats grasses" (Ps 106:20), this golden calf revered by an unfaithful people when Moses received the tab-lets of the covenant from the true God (Ex 32:19). "This girl is crazy," they said in the crowd. The newspapers stated: "Bernadette's place is in the asylum." Aunt Bernarde slapped you: "Stop this foolishness!" The ridicule continued. They treated you like a little "craphead."

Today, to me, your face is an icon of Jesus, who was beaten, whipped, and crowned with thorns, the suffering ser-vant who bears all our sins and who made himself become the antidote for the poison which was destroying our lives. Lord, innocent Lamb, to what limits your love for me drove you!

The herbs that Bernadette ate were also the symbol of the "bitter herbs" that the paschal lamb was stuffed with on the day of celebration of the liberation from Egypt. God freed his people from the yoke of the enemy who oppressed them— a cunning, inner enemy. The "cheap rosary, made of simple cord and black beads," Bernadette's rosary, which her mother brought back for her from a pilgrimage to Betharram, to me, suddenly becomes like the slingshot of the little David who was going to confront the giant Goliath. Prayer, when it brings me closer to the meaning of the crucifixion, is able to resolve the greatest difficulties of my soul. And I meditate, plunged into the mystery of the salvation of the world, with you, Bernadette, my little sister so close....

"It shouldn't bother you to kiss the ground for the sin-ners. It shouldn't bother you to walk on your knees for sin-ners. Penitence, penitence, penitence! It shouldn't bother you

to eat the herbs there for the sinners. Go and drink from the spring and wash yourself there." Bernadette, three times you rejected the muddy water before you drank. At Gethsemane, Jesus prayed three times to the Father: "My Father, if it is possible, let this cup pass from me....My Father, if this cannot pass unless I drink it, your will be done" (Mt 26:39, 42). And when they ask Bernadette why she did this, she explained with poise: *"Because the Lady told me to."*

Let us listen to the prophet Isaiah when he spoke of the humble servant: "For he grew up before him like a young plant...he had no form or majesty that we should look at him, nothing in his appearance that we should desire him. He was despised and rejected by others;...he has borne our infirmities and carried our diseases" (Isa 53:2–4).

And how could we not notice that the spring burst forth on the right side of the rock? The soldier's spear pierced the right side of Jesus on the cross, cutting through, in a transverse way, a lung, and then the heart. "At once blood and water came out" (Jn 19:34). I come to the realization, while writing these lines, that it was in the cavity situated up high to the left of the rock at Massabielle that Mary appeared, signifying symbolically the union of her heart and that of her son: the Heart of Jesus, where the Fathers of the Church have seen the source of all the sacraments, the Eucharist in particular, the crowning glory of baptism. "On that day a fountain shall be opened for the house of David...to cleanse them from sin and impurity" (Zech 13:1). "For they drank from the spiritual rock that followed them, and the rock was Christ" (1 Cor 10:4).

Am I blind for refusing to see the evidence of an infinite love that does nothing by chance and manifests itself in my own life? What is the date of my baptism? I want to remember it, like my own true birthday each year. Lord, open my eyes to the marvels of your presence. The baptismal fonts of the old parish church at Lourdes, where Bernadette was baptized, are the only things that are left of the old church. Lord, help me see the essential things amidst the ruins of the old world I have built for myself. Make me return to you and find the grace, once again, of my baptism, so that I can always be in the midst of an act of thanksgiving....The great biblical history of the people of God perseveres and I am a part of it. "The Lord said to Moses...'I will be standing there in front of you on the rock at Horeb. Strike the rock, and water will come out of it, so that the people may drink'" (Ex 17:5–6).

In God, there is no past and no future, there is only the present moment, lived in love. Lord, help me fully live each moment of the present, and drink your Word like a continuously renewing spring which quenches me along my road. Make the water always spring forth in my desert, torrents in my arid ground (Isaiah 15:4–7). "He brought me back to the entrance of the temple; there, water was flowing from below the threshold toward the east, the water was flowing down...and everywhere the water goes, life springs forth...because the water flows from the sanctuary" (Ezek 47:1, 9, 12).

But baptism doesn't stop with water, it continues with the gift of the Holy Spirit. Bernadette is going to be sent to build a Church to take her place there. The Church is all of us, and I am responsible for it. Through baptism, I am a priest, I am a prophet, I am a king! Thank you, Lord, for having made me rich in faith, an heir to the kingdom promised to those who love you. On the ramparts of the new Jerusalem, I want to be a sentinel (Isaiah 62:6). Day and night, I will never be silent! For the sake of the gospel, I will not be silent, I will never rest, Lord, until your justice springs forth like a beacon of light and your salvation like a burning torch!

REFLECTION QUESTIONS

Do the promises I made (or were made by my godparents in my name) at baptism still serve as the foundation of my faith? Am I ready to follow the path that God has set before me, regardless of how difficult it might appear? Am I prepared to serve God's will, even if that means appearing as a fool in the eyes of the world?

Loving the Church, the Body of Which I am a Member

FOCUS POINT

Indeed, the body does not consist of one member but of many....God arranged the members in the body, each one of them, as he chose....Now you are the body of Christ and individually members of it. And God has appointed in the church first apostles, second prophets, third teachers; then deeds of power, then gifts of healing, forms of assistance, forms of leadership, various kinds of tongues (1 Cor 12:14, 18, 27–28). I am a part of the Church, part of the Mystical Body of Christ.

"Go tell the priests to have a chapel built here and to have a procession."

B ernadette had promised to come for fifteen days. On the 27th of February, 800 people were at the grotto. On Sunday, the 28th, more than a thousand....The authorities were worried, and the Examining Magistrate, Ribes, summoned the visionary in order to dissuade her from continuing her visits to the grotto. She had already been summoned, the previous Thursday, to the office of the Imperial Prosecutor, Dutour (the one who had put François Soubirous into jail), and interrogated, while she stood with her mother at her side, for two hours. Louise was beginning to feel faint when they finally offered them two chairs, but Bernadette had refused: *"We will dirty them!"* She was not afraid of their threats, and their acts of intimidation failed to reach her in the general confusion. On the 21st of February, no one—not the Police Commissioner, Jacomet, nor the Imperial Prosecutor, nor the Examining Magistrate—could shake Bernadette's determination. She threw out the comment, *"I have been given the responsibility to tell you about it, I have not been given the responsibility to make you believe it,"* in order to cut short all controversy with the bothersome questioner. Jesus, when he was before the Sanhedrin and as well, before Pilate, had this same assurance, and later, the apostles themselves experienced it. Since then, all people, in whom God entrusts a particular mission, give witness to this magnificent internal freedom: love eradicates fear.

On the 1st of March, there was the same crowd, the same calm, and everyone was united with Bernadette in the penitential acts. There was a silent apparition, the only one in which a priest, Father Dézirat, was present. His disturbing report about the event demonstrated the total communion between Bernadette and Mary. It is a communion of spirit and heart that is offered to each one of us. This is the secret to "moving mountains"!

The movement to conversion which was begun astonished the local clergy, who were very wary. "If the reduction in acts of charity leaves the Church almost without true believers, miracles will reenergize it. This is one of the last effects of grace. If only a miracle would come to the Jesuits," commented Pascal in his *Pensées* (Thoughts), two centuries before these events....

On the first day of Saint Joseph's month, the first miracle at Lourdes took place. This would be retained by the Church, four years later, in order to officially recognize the apparitions. Catherine Latapie, who was nine months pregnant, came on foot from the village of Loubajac (some four miles from Lourdes) to bathe her paralyzed arm in the waters of the spring. When she left, she had been cured and, shortly after her arrival home, gave birth to the little Jean-Baptiste, who would later become a priest....

Now we come to March 2nd, the day of the thirteenth apparition. Once again, Bernadette heard the Lady say: *"Go tell the priests to build a chapel here and to have a procession."* Bernadette went, with her two aunts, Bernarde and Basile—who had been chased out of the Children of Mary for having become pregnant before marriage—to see the parish priest, Father Peyramale, in order to give him the request.... "Liar! It is unfortunate to have a family like this, which creates disorder in the parish!" he "shouts as if giving a sermon." The priest had forgotten the firm instructions given by his Lord and Master: "Take care that you do not despise one of these little ones; for, I tell you, in heaven their angels continually see the face of my Father" (Mt 18:10). Bernadette, who was not able, the same morning, to speak about anything except the procession, came back in the evening—accompanied by Dominiquette Cazenave, a good parishioner, the sister of the station master, François Soubirous' boss—in order to speak about the chapel. She would be questioned at the rectory by the entire parish clergy. She left, jumping for joy: *"I did my errand!"*

The meeting with the imposing parish priest—the son of an important family—shows Bernadette's extraordinary tenacity, her complete confidence in the Lady's message. *"Because she told it to me...."* She not only tells us that the Lord wants us to take part in his Church, but also that we are all called to build the Church together. In those days, the parish of Lourdes was placed under the patronage of Saint Peter. "...You are Peter, and on this rock, I will build my Church..." (Mt 16:18). This Church is not an administrative building, but the people, where each person has a role and holds a special place. On the morning of the Resurrection, Jesus chose Mary Magdalene, a laywoman—who had a checkered reputation—to communicate the good news! Bernadette, in that joyous morning, all people who were counseled and taught by Mary are profiled in you. The Church is you, me, all of us. It is not the local priest alone. Christians are the people chosen to give witness, everywhere, that God is love and he is only that!

"The lay person, before being a nonpriest or a nonreligious, is a baptized person who glorifies God, sanctifies himself in the world, and gives witness to the love of the Lord," explained Msgr. Coffy, at the Roman synod devoted to lay people, held in the Fall of 1987. That is a secret we can cry out from the rooftops! Not only can nothing push me aside in the Church—a people in action—where I am at home, but even more than that, the mission depends upon me, and we must say that! Was it not the "yes" of a young girl of about fourteen who decided the Incarnation of the Son? To put the

Word into action, who is better than she to show me the way?

Lord, with Mary and Bernadette—small, fragile, and powerless—you made Lourdes become the greatest pilgrimage center in the world. You want to do great things with me, as well. Here is my own "yes," given without reservation or restraint. Take it, use this "yes" for the best. I trust you and I want to love the Church, your Body, my people, my family... my heart's homeland!

Bernadette, like Moses, who was accompanied by his brother, Aaron, to go see Pharaoh, you did not want to be alone in your messenger duty. *"To build a chapel,"* is not just the act of placing stone upon stone, it is the act of gathering together a people in action, in *"procession."*

Lord, I remember that you asked Moses to build a sanctuary where the Ark of the Covenant would be placed: "Have them make me a sanctuary, so that I may dwell among them. In accordance with all that I show you concerning the pattern of the tabernacle and of all its furniture, so you shall make it" (Ex 25:8–9).

Mary is also the Ark of the Covenant in the Litanies of the Virgin.... How can we not see, anew, through the stories of the apparitions at Lourdes, the actualization of a holy parable about the people of God?

Since the episode when Jesus was lost and found again in the Temple, "the house of his Father," I know that all our temples of stone only have meaning as a function of this presence of Christ in us, with us, for us. May Saint Joseph, a carpenter, the patron saint of builders, teach me to build the temple, where God dwells, out of my own life surroundings. The true sanctuary is my heart, the world where I live in the light of *"the next world...."* That is the meaning we can give to this "chapel" at Massabielle, built near a place of disdain (the "pigpen"), apart from the old clerical structures and of a certain dominical Pharisaism. The Virgin Mary wanted this chapel, *"even a small one,"* said Bernadette. She wanted it to serve the Holy Spirit, who makes everything new again, so that our existence surprises us. And when we come there, in a procession, we do so to put ourselves on the right path to conversion: to live love daily, like in Nazareth!

Jesus Christ, you are the son of David, according to the Book of Kings in the Old Testament. "God said to David, 'Your son, whom I will set on your throne in your place, shall build the house for my name'" (1 Kings 5:5). It wasn't Solomon who built the Temple, it was you, Jesus, you, whose body is the true Temple, the Body of which I am a member, this part of humanity where the happiness of loving is experienced and grows....

REFLECTION QUESTIONS

Am I called by God to strengthen this Mystical Body of Christ, this people of God, through love and good works? What are the gifts, the talents, with which God has graced me? How can I use these talents to strengthen the Mystical Body of Christ of which I am a member?

An Answer to an Age-Old Question

FOCUS POINT

Like a small child who is unable to understand the words of his mother but who knows the love she has for him, there are times in prayer when I cannot discern God's meaning but am well aware of the depth of his love for me. Sometimes it is not so much what is said as how it is spoken, with what intention, and the love that is present within it.

"I am the Immaculate Conception."

They wanted to keep Bernadette away from the grotto: neither the authorities, nor the detractors, and not even pressure tactics bothered her. *"Que bouï ana...I want to go there."* The last of the fifteen days fell on Thursday, the 4th of March. In the same way as for his Incarnation, the Lord chose a woman for great things.

"For a third time, I went to find the parish priest to tell him that the Lady had ordered me to go tell the priests to have a chapel built there. He looked at me for a moment and then asked me, in a rather unsuitable tone: 'Who is this lady?' I answered that I didn't know. Then, he gave me the task to ask her what her name was and then come back and tell it to him. The following day, when I arrived at the grotto, after having said my rosary, I asked her, on behalf of the parish priest, what her name was, but all she did was smile. Upon returning, I went to see the parish priest to tell him I had done what he had asked of me but that her only answer had been a smile. Then he said she was making fun of me and that it was better for me not to return to the grotto, but I was not able to stop myself from going there...."

Bernadette went to see Father Peyramale, *"the parish priest,"* on the 2nd, 3rd, and 4th of March in order to transmit the message from *Aquero* concerning the procession and the chapel. "Make her tell you her name and cause the rosebush to flower" was his answer (these were his conditions for building the chapel). The "fifteen days" of meetings with the Lady had ended without the young lady of the grotto ever revealing her identity. Bernadette returned to school and continued to prepare for her first Communion.

On the 25th of March, the feast of the Annunciation, Bernadette's inner call to go to the grotto took precedence over her will to be obedient.

"I asked her three times in a row. She continued to smile. Finally, I dared to ask a fourth time. While extending her arms, she lifted her eyes up to heaven. Then she joins her hands in prayer, bringing them up to her breast and told me that she was the Immaculate Conception. These were the last words she said to me. Once again, I went to see the parish priest to tell him she had told me that she was the Immaculate Conception. He asked me if I was certain of this. I told him I was and that I had repeated her final words to myself all the way back so that I would not forget them."

Bernadette had heard the name in patois (the local dialect): *"Que soy era Immaculada Councepciou (I am the Immaculate Conception)."* Peyramale was shocked and held back a sob. In a letter to the bishop that same evening, he wrote: "She could not have made this up!" This apparition had very far-reaching implications. Thursday, March the 4th had been the last day of the fifteen-day meetings. There had been a large crowd at the grotto which had come away disappointed because no visible "sign" seemed to have been given....We must not give ultimatums to God. We must ensure that our prayers don't take the same form as registered letters, requesting a confirmation of receipt! God speaks to us through whatever voice he chooses, if he chooses to do so, and when he chooses. Let us make ourselves available, attentive, and receptive. But it is he who loves us first. It is he who comes to us.

The Lady named herself, but only after the fourth request, by means of an expressive gesture of lifting her eyes to heaven, as if to receive the message of who she was: *"I am the Immaculate Conception."*

Bernadette, you did not understand the meaning of that phrase until Mr. Estrade, a local businessman, explained it to you that same evening. I can only imagine your joy! It is also the same joy I experience when I figure out, thanks to a close friend, what God wants to say to me in a certain situation I have experienced. Help me hear what is said to me, today, on God's behalf. Intercede on my behalf so that my heart is truly open to listen....

The disclosure of the Divine Name was completely unexpected. Marie Duffo, who related the story the following day to her younger brother, a boarder at Saint Pé, understood it to mean: "I am the Immaculate Virgin." But the reality behind the Divine Name was more telling. Less than four years prior to this, on December 8, 1854, Pope Pius IX had proclaimed the dogma of the Immaculate Conception. The Divine Name that had been revealed in Lourdes was the answer that had been awaited for centuries. The Immaculate Conception, so great, so close: the perfect symbol of the mystery of God of which she was the masterpiece. The blood of Christ brings us the splendor of the beginning.

My entire lifetime will not give me enough time to express my thanksgiving! May my prayer be one of praise. Through Mary, I can be reborn in Christ. If I allow myself to be spiritually fascinated by her, a new man will be born and will grow. The time has come for me, with Saint Louis Marie Grignion, to say, with all my heart, this prayer of consecration: "Today, I choose you, O Mary, in the presence of the entire celestial court, to be my mother and my queen. To you, in total submission and love, I give my body, my soul, all my interior and exterior goods, and even the value of my good actions, past, present, and future, granting you the total and complete right to use me and all that belongs to me, without exception, as you choose fit, for the greater glory of God, now and for all eternity. Amen." Bernadette lived this personal consecration even without expressing it in this same manner, but I am convinced that she could assent to it.

Mary Immaculate, you are the springtime of the world, the blossoming of humanity, the sunny summit of the tree with a thousand bruised roots. You are a woman, beaming with love. Through you, both the history of the world, as well as my own, renews itself today because when you dwell in a soul, the Holy Spirit also enters!

The archangel Gabriel gave you a new name on the morning of the Annunciation: "Filled with Grace." And it is in celebration of this day that you choose to name yourself for Bernadette and for us all. Bernadette's parents were there with their little one, at 4:00 A.M. on the 25th of March, when she received that gentle call, which she recognized, profoundly in her heart.

Do these calls from the Holy Spirit resound within me? Are they not smothered by my preoccupations, my secondhand information? Lord, I want to remain silent so that I can live in unison with your presence and your will for me.

Today, these words from Exodus come to mind: "If I come to the Israelites and say to them, 'The God of your ancestors has sent me to you,' and they ask me: 'What is his name?' what shall I say to them? God said to Moses: 'I AM WHO I AM'" (3:13–14). Perhaps Moses no longer understood the Lord's answer, perhaps Bernadette didn't understand the Lady's answer....When the Creator manifests himself, without an intermediary, through the voice of a new creation, he does so because he wants to bring us into the adventure of rebirth.

Mary, you are the spiritual model through which I can

find myself and also my new name, the one written on the white stone of Revelation (2:17), this name which will allow me, when it is my turn, to become "Emmanuel," God within us, the one who carries his presence everywhere....

Bernadette, without knowing it, you gazed upon the burning bush that Moses saw in the desert. You have seen the earth illuminated by the light of God. And you bring us to an awareness of our misery, you call us to the desert. "When you have brought the people out of Egypt, you shall worship God on this mountain" (Ex 3:12). Along with you, I hope to let Mary gaze upon me, she who is God's messenger, she who carried him in her womb. She wasn't alone in the grotto, she was pregnant—it was the Annunciation, the first day of the time that took her to childbirth—filled with the One who would offer himself to me as living bread....

May my prayer become a loving dialogue with the Lord who spoke to Moses, "face to face, as one speaks to a friend" (Ex 33:11). *The Lady smiled at me*—Bernadette said—*she looked at me as one person looks at another person.*

The new Eve, without sin, is a person like me, "filled with a light which preceded her and encircles her, a light that does not come from her directly but which, however, gives her all of her substance" (André Cabes). This welcomed light helps me evolve from a single individual—concerned only with himself—to a blossomed person, living in communion with others, "full of grace," in whom God can see and recognize himself! To be a mirror for God, that is my vocation, the essential call of the Holy Spirit, sent to my heart....

In effect, Immaculate Mary, who are you, if not the One in whom heaven and earth are united, all eternal love with all created love? Through you, God-made-man took shape and developed, bringing us along with him to live at the very heart of the Blessed Trinity for all eternity. The Holy Spirit, the personal expression and fruit of the reciprocal love of the Father and the Son, lives in your soul, Immaculate Virgin.... The Lord made the Word-of-God-made-flesh, Jesus Christ, come to life through you. The very close union of love that unites you with the Holy Spirit is like the union between a wife and a husband. Therefore, in a way, Mary, it was the name of the Holy Spirit you gave us, by presenting yourself in Lourdes! I may be exaggerating a little, being strongly influenced by Saint Maximilian Kolbe's ideas, but the supposition is a fair one. "The offering of oneself to the Immaculate Conception: we must be her children, we must be hers in all ways until we become a part of her very self," wrote the enflaming saint.

These profound reflections make me dizzy and I am taking the risk of becoming discouraged when faced with the magnitude of the mystery. But I believe that the Immaculate Conception reveals the ultimate of the realization of man to each one of us. Far from making me feel as if I am a stranger to the relationship between the Virgin Mary and the Holy Spirit, in it, I can see the supreme example of my vocation to love, through the giving of myself in response to the love of God. Love should be the principal source and motivation behind my actions: there it is, the law and the prophets! Everything else is lip service.

May my prayer simply be an invitation to the Holy Spirit in order that my life will be a fervent invocation so that this gathering of nations, in the splendor of the Dawn, becomes the Body of Christ. "Blessed be the God and Father of our Lord Jesus Christ....He chose us...to be holy and blameless before him in love" (Eph 1:3–4). The consequence of our baptism is our divinization. Raised from the dead with Christ, we are deified with him. Baptized in Christ, we have a new name, the one which Mary was the first to carry, but one which we all carry with her: "Immaculate."

"Mary's epiphany at Lourdes intervenes like a summation and a new wellspring. The Church now recognizes who the Mother of the Lord is and what her mission is: her name is her mission, the Immaculate Conception, the seed and the promise of the Kingdom" (André Cabes, *Mary, the Path of Living Water*).

REFLECTION QUESTIONS

Do I welcome the love of God into my heart even though I am unable to completely understand his will and plan for my life? Am I trusting enough of Jesus to love him in spite of my fears and the many distractions that clamor for my attention? Am I able to pray to God without words, without concepts, and simply enjoy his presence?

Living the Eucharist

FOCUS POINT

While they were eating, Jesus took a loaf of bread, and after blessing it he broke it, gave it to the disciples, and said, "Take, eat; this is my body." Then he took a cup , and after giving thanks he gave it to them, saying, "Drink from it, all of you; for this is my blood of the covenant, which is poured out for many for the forgiveness of sins. I tell you, I will never again drink of this fruit of the vine until that day when I drink it new with you in my Father's kingdom." (Mt 26:26–29)

"What made you happier, your first Communion or the apparitions?"
"These two things go together and can't be compared. I was very happy about the two of them."

Bernadette answers a friend

On the 27th of March, three doctors examined Bernadette, acting on the orders of the prefect. They found nothing to justify her hospitalization. Decidedly, this girl was not insane! Easter fell on the 6th of April: Bernadette participated very simply with great happiness in her heart. On Wednesday, the 7th of April, which was the following day, she again felt the inner call. She ran to the grotto with a large candle (one which was too big to carry for a long time, but large enough to stand on its own on the ground). While she was in her ecstasy (as she experienced what she called "ecstasy" during the apparitions), she didn't notice that the lit candle had slipped while in her enjoined hands and, for a period of ten minutes, the flames licked her fingers…without burning her! Doctor Dozous examined these two small hands and began to believe in the apparitions. This "miracle of the candle" happened on Easter Wednesday. Bernadette's death, some twenty-one years later, would also occur on an Easter Wednesday. And in death, her body would be left untouched in the same way as the flame of the lit candle had left her hands unburned. In effect, Bernadette's body remains, today, incorrupt, as if awaiting the great morning of the Resurrection….

This seventeenth meeting with the Virgin Mary had been silent. Is it not true that the signs we receive in our lives speak to us louder than words? Here, we see the sign of fire, one of the four elements present in Lourdes, along with stone (the ground), water, and air (the wind). Some people search for a fifth element. Would it not be the Eucharist, the God of Love made real…in order to sanctify everything? In fact, Bernadette would later make her first Communion during the period of the apparitions.

The parish priest, Father Peyramale, was amazed by the new fervor in his parish and the changes in Bernadette made him speak in favor of the apparitions. He confided to the bishop: "Everything that happens to her does so in an astonishing way." She received Jesus through the Eucharist, for the first time, on June 3rd, the feast of the Body of Christ (Corpus Christi). She had so desired that moment! She was asked if her happiness was as great as when she saw the Blessed Virgin and she answered: *"These two things go together and can't be compared. I was very happy about the two of them."* Why is this? In both cases, the experience is hidden with Christ in God, like the apostle Paul said in his letter to the Colossians. Only those who learn to be reborn with Christ, by living their baptism, can be mysteriously introduced into it. That is exactly what Mary had referred to as the *"next world"* on the 18th of February.... Bernadette was entering into it more and more: the experience of the Eucharist crowned the apparitions in a secret way. In fact, continuously, since the third apparition, Bernadette was accompanied by the experience of the candle and its flame, the symbol of Christ, resurrected on Easter night. Christ, who took upon himself all the sins of the world.

Bernadette, your prayer is essentially Christ's prayer, a prayer with Christ in prayer.... From the 3rd of June, 1858, onwards, the Host in all the Masses and all your Communions was Jesus the Savior, who associated you with his mission through the intermediary Mary: *"Pray and make others pray for the sinners."*

What place does the Eucharist have in my life? Am I hungry for this bread? Lord, may Bernadette's own example push me to want to receive you through this sacrament every day, this sign which represents the realization of my progressive transformation into a new person. Just as the mountain rabbits turn white in the snow...I am called, in the same way, to become what I have received, God-made-man through Christ! My faith is not strong enough. I always make excuses not to go to meet you, Jesus-Eucharist. Some other "task" detracts me. I have important things to do...and I am dying, little by little, I am falling into ruin without even knowing it. My life resembles those villages built as sets for the movies—cardboard facades held up artificially by scaffolds of vanity.

Let us listen to Bernadette's advice—when she had become Sister Marie Bernard—given to her little cousins as they were preparing to make their first Communion (around 1875): *"When our Lord will be in your heart, give yourself up to him completely and, in peace, savor the delicious taste of his presence. Love, adore, listen, praise, I will even say 'rejoice.'"* Rejoice? That is not necessarily our experience with the Eucharist, especially at Sunday Mass. The elderly ladies who "shush" the little ones, others who dig into their wallets, searching for that quarter to give at collection time...and me, when I get discouraged at the length of the sermon...this is a sad picture of a regular reality today. Nevertheless, there are certainly ways to live the Eucharist otherwise, in more depth and in a more "expressive" way—like a loving meeting— perhaps during the week, early in the morning, or in the evening, after work.

To Pierre, her little brother and godson, as he was preparing to make his first Communion, Sister Marie Bernard wrote: *"The angels, who possess this God, who is three times Holy, incessantly singing his praises, already envy your happiness because they cannot, like us, receive him....What kindness on Jesus' part to descend down to us to the point of giving himself to us and making us his dwelling place"* (May 23, 1872). Bernadette, support me in the desire to thirst and hunger for this supernatural strength, an all-powerful Love which redeems the world, that opens our souls like the sails of a ship on the vast sea, and makes us all gods in blossom....

In her notebook, where she recopied phrases she had heard or read, Bernadette noted: *"I am nothing and out of this nothing, Jesus made something great. Yes, realizing that, in a way, I am a God through holy Communion."*

From Bernadette's precise testimonials, it has come out that Mary, at Massabielle, taught her a secret prayer and confided three secrets to her, of which nothing specific has ever come to light. These were only with reference to the messenger and were given to help her grow in faith. Bernadette's great secret was her mysterious union with the crucified Christ, most particularly through the Eucharist, which plunges us to the core of Trinitarian love. Later, ill, having become a religious, she will suffer from not having been able to attend Mass as often as she would have liked and at other times, for long periods, like from October of 1875 to May of 1876. To appease her hunger for the Eucharist a little, onto the curtains of her little alcove, she pinned a picture showing a priest lifting the consecrated Host, and during her periods of insomnia, she used this to unite her spirit with other Masses being said around the world....

The Eucharist transforms me gently, in "natural doses," giving me a small foretaste of heaven. Bernadette remarked: *"The soul takes only one path, from Golgotha to Mount Tabor. It leaves Golgotha to go to Mount Tabor to seek strength and courage. Life is the ladder...."*

REFLECTION QUESTIONS

Am I attentive to the presence of Jesus Christ in the Eucharist when I receive the Blessed Sacrament? Am I filled with awe and excitement when I consume the body and blood of our Lord and Savior? Am I transformed by the "bread of life" to the point of becoming a new person, one who sees with new eyes the love of God, one who loves as God loves?

From the Garden of Olives to Tabor

FOCUS POINT

Then Peter said in reply, "Look we have left everything and followed you. What then will we have?" Jesus said to them, "Truly I tell you, at the renewal of all things, when the Son of Man is seated on the throne of his glory, you who have followed me will also sit on twelve thrones, judging the twelve tribes of Israel. And everyone who has left houses or brothers or sisters or father or mother or children or fields, for my name's sake, will receive a hundredfold, and will inherit eternal life. But many who are first will be last, and the last will be first" (Mt 19:27–30).

"I saw no barriers…she was more beautiful than ever."

A period of a hundred days passed between the second-to-last apparition and the final one, which occurred on the 16th of July, 1858, the feast day of Our Lady of Mount Carmel. Bernadette received the inner call to go to Massabielle, but the way to the grotto had been blocked with barriers. Bernadette waited until the evening. Secretly, accompanied by her young aunt, Lucile Castérot, Bernadette ran to her encounter, disguised as a pilgrim. She placed herself on the other side of the river Gave, in the field, at sunset, around 8:00 P.M. The Virgin seemed to be very close by. She said nothing and Bernadette understood this to be her farewell....

Everything had begun in front of the grotto, much in the same way as in the story of the prophet Elijah, the major inspiration for Carmel. He felt that God was close to him in a light gust of wind, in front of a grotto in Horeb. No one before him, except Moses, had felt this. This was exactly the same way that the apparitions of Our Lady at Lourdes had begun. We know that the name "Carmel" is taken from the mountain where the prophet Elijah lived, and where the first crusaders looked for traces of him. Then Lourdes appears. Is it, perhaps, a new Carmel, a new holy mountain? Yes, it invites us to transform our own homes into a retreat in the middle of the world, it asks us not to wear the cross simply as a piece of decorative jewelry, but to carry such a secret of the love that transforms in the very depth of our hearts.

All our "pigpens" can become exalted places of Trinitarian presence if we enter into a relationship with God, he who always takes the first steps for a meeting and for whom no true barrier exists. This eighteenth apparition is the final one. Bernadette said: *"I saw no barriers, she was more beautiful than ever...."*

In my life, there are many obstacles placed on my road to

a meeting with the Lord: noise, worries.... But I learn how to pray in all conditions, in the subway and on the bus, for example, by contemplating on the faces which become like living icons to me.... My great desire, Lord, is to pray endlessly, to remain connected with you, to bask a little in your love, there, where nothing is expected. If I am baptized and pray only in church or in my room, am I truly a missionary? I must bring peace and forgiveness into those places which are the most hostile towards you, my Lord. If possible, I am to do so without words, using only my actions and by sending small "messages of love" to others through my thoughts....

The last apparition occurred under unfavorable conditions—barriers—when the sun was setting. However, the forces of good laugh at the walls built between our souls and their wellspring. My relationship with God is not hindered by the machinations of separation and division: the wood of the cross in all its manifestations. My relationship is even more beautiful during these difficult times if I take the means to discreetly make contact with the *"next world,"* sometimes, simply with a small invocation.

My key to reestablishing communication with the Lord when I feel that barriers are being erected and when I run the risk of losing my faith is: "Jesus, Savior, come to my aid, I love you." With Bernadette, I go, like she said, from the *"Garden of Olives"*—the place of agony—to Tabor. Does Bernadette not follow in the wake of Moses and Elijah, the two prophets who were witnesses to the Transfiguration of the Lord (Mk 9:2–8)?

Tabor's climate of peace and quiet harmony also characterized Jesus' childhood. It is as if I was finally entering into the world of the Incarnation, in Nazareth, in Tabor, where God-made-man demonstrated that his Word enlightens all the concrete aspects of my life. Saint Joseph tells me, in the same way as the angel told him: "Do not be afraid to accept Mary into your home." She will teach me how to walk in the path of the gospel, in the same way as she taught her son. She will make me aware of my importance as a son through the Son.

Like the little cloud preceded the large one on Mount Carmel, heralding the end of the drought (1 Kings 18:41–46), the Virgin Mary left Lourdes, on the 16th of July, 1858, leaving all of it to Christ. This is a rather loose interpretation but the message of Lourdes is fathomless, like God's grace. There, each of us can draw what the Holy Spirit wants to give to us....The Book of Revelation seems to be summarized in the message from Lourdes, like a little book, opened at the threshold of the third millennium. In Lourdes, the Bible regains its weight of truth in my life. This old "adventure" involves me!

One thing is certain, God looks for me in the garden of signs, like he looked for Adam in the Garden of Eden: "Where are you?" Mary represents us all through her response to the love of God. She is truly the mother of the new humanity who allow themselves to be loved by their creator. Let us listen to the Song of Solomon, where everything is said about this ardent search: "My Beloved speaks and says to me: 'Arise, my love, my fair one, and come away.... O my dove, in the clefts of the rock, in the covert of the cliff, let me see your face, let me hear your voice...'" (Song 2:10, 14).

Lourdes really illustrates this verse! The cleft of the rock is, at the same time, the retreat where the dove hides itself and the opening in the side of the Husband through which he reveals himself....

Let us think about the thrust of the spear that split his side, from which blood and water flowed. This is the place where I am born to the new life. Lord Jesus, by drinking at this "spiritual rock that follows me" (1 Cor 10:4), I find that the wound in your heart is the place where I can strengthen my hope. I would not like to hide myself anywhere else! Today, with Bernadette, with no false modesty or losing time through reasoning, I would like to say: *"Divine heart of my Jesus, give me the gift to always love you more and more. In my despair, I will find kindness and patience in Jesus' heart. I will find true consolation there."*

These are ancient words, but the love behind them is new. Strengthened by this love, I will go from prayers to the ultimate prayer, from the church made of stone—the building destined for destruction—to Peter's Church: one, holy, universal, and cosmic! My heart opens itself to all the dimensions of God's heart and I will be able to love without measure, beyond everything else. I want to love like the overflowing heart of God. I am like a vessel at the well, and my heart overflows with yours, Bernadette....

My cup is full and I give thanks! In the *"Journal dédié à la Reine du Ciel"* (Journal Dedicated to the Queen of Heaven), Bernadette said: *"O tender Mother, make it so that your child imitates you in everything and for everything, and in a word, make it so that I will be a child in your heart and that of your cherished Son."* This was written in Lourdes, in May 1866, at a time when she prayed to obtain the virtue of humility—a virtue she requested every day. It is a virtue I should request at least as often as that, if I truly want to follow the evangelical example set by both Bernadette and Mary....

It is wonderful to discover that the parish of Lourdes has, since the time of the apparitions, become the parish of the Sacred Heart. Mary leads me to the single source of happiness and salvation. It is by nourishing ourselves with the blood of her heart that the Heart of Christ is formed. This spiritual reality continues until the end of time. It is a mystery which envelops and carries me from this world to the next, at the same slow pace as the germinations which produce our marvelous springtimes. Lord, the wheat grows in me, waiting for the time when its grain will be ground, when it dies. That will be another stage, the most fruitful one. I prepare myself for it. But I want to die armed, lovingly holding the spear of the living Word firmly in my hand.... I begin today with a smile which will take me to Mary's side to become her face of tenderness, to work with her on her mission of reconciliation and unity, given to the Church in this developing world. Bernadette, carry me in your wake, so I can love like Mary, allowing myself to be chosen and "espoused" by the Holy Spirit, to welcome the Word of God so that I can carry it within me—in my heart—and through my actions, give birth to it.

REFLECTION QUESTIONS

Are there barriers in my life preventing me from a full relationship with Jesus? What are these obstacles and distractions? Do I pray for God's grace and the strength to overcome these barriers?

DAY TEN

The Rock That Is
My Salvation

"I will show you what someone is like who comes to me, hears my words, and acts on them. That one is like a man building a house, who dug deeply and laid the foundation on rock; when a flood arose, the river burst against that house but could not shake it, because it had been well built" (Lk 6:47–48).

"The grotto, that was my heaven."

E ight years after the apparitions, on the 3rd of July, 1866, Bernadette went to the grotto for a final prayer, a final kiss to the rock. *"The grotto, that was my heaven."* She left the next day for the Saint Gildard convent, having joined the Sisters of Charity at Nevers. What happened during these eight years?

The Soubirous family had left the unsanitary "cachot" in the month of May, 1858, to move to a room in the home of Deluc, the baker. Bernadette had been subjected to many endless visits and had already been harassed by the "paparazzi"! Being the first to live the message of penitence, she had no desire to play the role of the star that they wanted her to.

She was confirmed, in the parish church, by Msgr. Laurence, on the 5th of February, 1860. The bishop met her that day in the sacristy. On the 15th of February, 1860, Father Peyramale entrusted Bernadette to the Sisters of the Hospice as a boarder. There she had peace, and the school was in the same building....On the 18th of January, 1862, after a long inquiry, the bishop of Tarbes published a pastoral letter, stating his findings about the events at Lourdes. Eight hundred years earlier, in 1062, by means of an official act, Count Bernard the First of Bigorre had given the county as a donation to the Virgin and, by so doing, enjoined his successors to honor this "suzerain state." The text of this act, in Latin, is preserved at the Bigorre chartulary, in the Pau archives, where I was able to consult it, with great emotion. The document is rarely brought up, but in my heart, I feel it has its own importance.

The legend concerning the founding of Lourdes states that Charlemagne, around the year 778, when he was returning from Spain, mounted a siege on the Mirambel castle which was held by Mirat, the Muslim chief. The Saracen (Muslim) finally gave himself to our Lady, represented by the bishop of Puy, who baptized him and gave him the name "Lores," from which the name "Lourdes" originates.

Whatever happened, we are able to accept the idea that the Virgin had seen Lourdes as her home for a long time. The "suzerain" had come to a territory which had been entrusted to her. She had heard the prayers of Bernard the First and his wife, Clémence! From the time of Bernard the First to Bernadette, Bigorre, a Marian land, had, therefore, been destined to welcome the message of the Virgin. Let us be aware that our prayers of dedication, our offertory acts to his benevolent love, and all our requests are taken seriously by God!

This pastoral letter, written by Msgr. Laurence, which designated the grotto as a blessed and venerated site, by recognizing the apparitions to be "true," would have far-reaching consequences: Our Lady of Lourdes would be the only "apparition" celebrated annually, on February 11th, in the universal church calendar. The text of this pastoral letter is beautiful and powerful, the pastor had difficulty containing his enthusiasm.

> The testimony of the young lady gives us all the guarantees we could ever want. First and foremost, her sincerity cannot be questioned. Whoever knew her, could only admire the simplicity, candor, and the modesty of this child. When everyone was dwelling on the marvels that were revealed to her, only she was silent: she only spoke when she was questioned. In response, she related everything without pretense or hesitation, with a touching innocence. To the numerous questions asked of her, she gave clear and precise answers, right to the point, which were marked by a strong conviction.... Never wavering in all of the interrogations we subjected her to, she constantly upheld what she had said, never adding or retracting

anything....But if Bernadette did not intend to mislead, did she not fool herself? Had she been the victim of a hallucination? How could we believe that? The wisdom of her answers revealed that this child was of righteous spirit, had a calm imagination, and common sense beyond her years. The religious feeling never showed her to be of exalted character. We have determined that this young woman had no intellectual disorder, no mental impairment, no character abnormalities, and no taste for the morbid which could have disposed her to imaginary creations. She didn't only see it once, but eighteen times....We find that the Immaculate Mary, Mother of God, truly appeared to Bernadette on the 11th of February, 1858, and on the days that followed; a total of eighteen times. We find that this apparition has all the aspects of truth, and that the faithful are fully justified to believe in it.

It is said, it is written. It is official and definite!

Bernadette, in this portrait that the bishop of Tarbes has created of you, we can find a number of paths our life can follow: simplicity, silence, agreement with oneself, righteous spirit.... These qualities are the fruit of your prayer: the Holy Spirit embraces you! In 1858, you only knew how to say your rosary. When you met the Lady, you remained silent, waiting in front of the grotto. I also want to pray in this manner: silently awaiting God, no matter where I find myself. This grotto was the most ill-reputed place in Lourdes: "the pigpen," where no one went. However, the pork farmer took his animals there every day! Dead wood, animal carcasses, and a variety of debris were piled up there. Couples held clandestine meetings there.... Our Lady, Mary, through her singular intermediary, Bernadette, made it one of the most attractive places.... Even nonChristians like to go to pray there. We have even built replicas of this place all over the world.

Msgr. Laurence purchased the bare rock of the present-day site of the Stations of the Cross at the end of November, 1869, just before he left for the First Vatican Council in Rome (where he died in 1870). A hundred years later, this place has become a garden of incomparable beauty, with its beautiful oak trees, and the grandest of beech trees....

Regardless of however poor our life may be, God can do wonders with the ungrateful soil we think we are, just as he did with the humble Bernadette. Let nothing discourage us, because nothing can separate us from God's love! Don't be afraid to be saints: "All things work together for good for those who love God" (Rom 8:28), even our mistakes!

The Book of Psalms tells us that the Lord is the rock of our salvation (18:2; 31:3; 71:3). Our rock is Christ! Don't forget these words which Bernadette wrote to her sisters in Lourdes when she arrived in Nevers, in July of 1866: *"I beg you to be so good as to offer some prayers when you go to the grotto: you will find me there, in spirit, attached to the foot of the rock I love so much...."*

To be attached to this rock is to pray, like Mary—the sister of Martha—at Christ's feet. We cannot understand the gospel without being prayerful. There, where the exegetist and the sage can no longer understand, the prayerful sees. Love speaks....

The waters of life spring from this rock of salvation. "Let anyone who is thirsty come to me, and let the one who believes in me drink" (Jn 7:37–38). The Holy Spirit and the bride echo this in the Book of Revelation: "Let everyone who is thirsty come. Let anyone who wishes take the water of life as a gift" (22:17). This water is "the Holy Spirit who will receive those have believed in him," explains the apostle John....

To never thirst again! I would like to never again thirst for recognition, power, or material goods. Lord, today I ask you for the grace to be able to remain attached to you, like a rock, so that your Holy Spirit will introduce me into the all-encompassing truth.

Lord Jesus, you and the Father are one (Jn 10:30). To belong to you in the Holy Spirit is to live united with the Father from whom all blessings flow. What more could I ask? To do the will of God, to love as he loves.... "In order to see God's will, we must love. Love is clairvoyant; it sees everything; it understands everything, it anticipates, it tells all," said Michel Garicoïts, the little barefooted Basque shepherd who became an apostle to the will of God, fulfilled with love and canonized in 1947. He was the founder of an order of priests whose only program was the one in Jesus' Heart. He had a profound effect on the Soubirous family, whom he frequently visited, coming from the nearby Marian Sanctuary in Betharram. His only motto was: "God, I have come to do your will" (Heb 10:7), to which he added: "Without delay, without reservation, without expectation for return, through love."

Bernadette, help me so that I am not satisfied simply by good feelings. "Oh well my child, you were lucky, the Blessed Virgin promised you heaven!" Faced with these words from two religious when you were leaving Michel Garicoïts' house—the charismatic saint from Betharram—around 1862, you replied: "Yes, if I earn it." You wanted to say that love is a never-ending battle, fought alongside Jesus on the cross. It is this battle which I want to pursue, relying on the rock that brings me my strength and faith.

With you, Bernadette, daughter of light, I want God's thoughts to become my own. May my faith bring splendor to life, may my prayer be alive and as simple as any everyday experience....

REFLECTION QUESTIONS

Is my life built upon a strong foundation, "the rock" that is God's love and guidance? Do storms of fear, pride, and temptation shake my faith to rubble? Or do I listen to the words of God and shape my life according to those words, so that obstacles and distraction are short-lived, holding no sway over my desire to do God's will?

DAY ELEVEN

Free to Say Yes

FOCUS POINT

An argument arose among them as to which one of them was the greatest. But Jesus, aware of their inner thoughts, took a little child and put it by his side, and said to them, "Whoever welcomes this child in my name welcomes me, and whoever welcomes me welcomes the one who sent me; for the least among all of you is the greatest" (Lk 9:46–48).

"Now, I am like everyone else."

Bernadette is happy that she is now just like everyone else. It was a sorry responsibility for her to have been obligated to answer the curiosity seekers who questioned her, unless they recognized themselves as sinners. *"Since you are a sinner"*: then she agreed to remake the Sign of the Cross of the Virgin and the gesture Mary made in proclaiming herself as the Immaculate Conception. This was a gesture that would move Msgr. Laurence, a dignified and stern man, to tears. Through obedience, Bernadette would learn to read, write, and speak French, not only her native patois.

"Now, I am like everyone else." She was searching for her vocation. Now free, she could not allow herself to be swept along where she did not want to go. She had made inquiries with Carmel, and went to the convent at Bagnères, but her health prevented her from entering there. She refused the monumental cornet of the Sisters of the Cross at Saint Pé of Bigorre, saying, *"I don't want any part of that tunnel!"*

On the 28th of April, 1862, Bernadette received the anointing of the sick. As soon as she had taken Communion, her breathing returned to normal, even though both of her lungs had been affected. On the 24th of September, 1865, Msgr. Forcade, the bishop of Nevers, questioned Bernadette about her future. He proposed that she enter the congregation of the Sisters of Nevers but she opposed this due to her heath, poverty, and lack of knowledge.... The authorities in the congregation did not welcome Msgr. Forcade's proposition with much enthusiasm, at least officially. The order has its rules, which the Lord accepts, for he has seen others! "She will be a permanent fixture in the infirmary, and, as well, she doesn't know how to do many things...."

At the end of March, 1864, Bernadette was very ill and on the 4th of April, decided to enter the congregation of the Sisters of Nevers. She was not able to attend the solemn inauguration of Fabisch's statue which was installed in the grotto. Anyway, she did not like this statue. In her opinion, the icon of the Virgin and Child at the Cambrai Cathedral most resembled *Aquero*—A Virgin and Child, a Virgin of tenderness, a treasure from the Orient, dating from the unified Church, crowned by Leo XIII in 1893. It is an icon which sparks us with a desire to choose unity today, with Mary, the Mother of us all....

The winter of 1865–66 passed without serious incident regarding Bernadette's health and she was authorized to request admission to the novitiate. On the 19th of May, at the request of Msgr. Laurence, she attended the inauguration of the crypt of the Lourdes Basilica. François, her beloved father, had worked on it. It was very difficult for Bernadette to pass there unnoticed. She prepared to leave, said farewell to her friends and, on the 3rd of July, went to the grotto one last time. The time for giving witness through words was finished.

Like each of us, Bernadette groped to understand what God expected from her. The Virgin Mary had neither revealed to her that she should become a religious, nor had she furthermore told her with which congregation. Her vocation was not part of the *"secrets"* which Mary entrusted to her. Above all, these concerned her personal relationship with God, her prayers. Someone said: "I know one of your secrets—it is that you will become a religious." She laughed and replied, *"It's more serious than that!"*

We do know that when the mayor of Lourdes suggested that she learn a trade, in 1858, she replied that she would like to be a religious. Above all, what she wanted was to be left in peace after all these extraordinary events. Without a doubt, Bernadette would have made a good mother. Her hand in marriage had been requested by Raoul de Tricqueville, a medical intern from Nantes, who had written to the bishop, considering him, morally, to be like a father to the young girl. Were these letters ever shown to her? If marriage is considered a sacrament, this would have been a holy vocation for her as well. It would not have been considered as having been a lesser spiritual vocation. Hadn't Mary herself been married? In reality, the problem is not only the life choices I make, it is in my desire to live in the presence of God, in his light, and to respond to the personal call he sends me. "God wants us to be saints because we belong to him," volunteered Father Fernand Barraque, a witness to the faith at the Lourdes Sanctuary. Whether I am a religious, married, or no matter what else, only love matters! "My vocation, finally I found it, my vocation is love": I believe that the words of Thérèse of the Child Jesus—a Doctor of the Church—could also be Bernadette's own words.

From the age of sixteen to twenty-two, Bernadette lived at the hospice of the Sisters of Nevers. She had seen nothing else, or practically nothing. *"I love the poor a great deal, I love taking care of the sick, I will stay with the Sisters of Nevers."* She dedicated herself to the religious life through love. A commitment such as this was rare in a time when certain young girls from good families were placed in religious vocations serving almost as celestial insurance policies for their parents....

What is certain is that Bernadette wanted to hide herself so that she could be like everyone else and that she let herself be guided by love in making her free choice. She loved the poor and the sick. The motto of this congregation could be summed up as: *"Deus charitas est,"* "God is love," attested to by a stained-glass window in the Saint Gildard Convent, in Nevers. If she had undertaken marriage, she would have loved in the same way.

Today, what does my desire to love amount to? Does my heart burn with love for God, who I meet through others? Am I attached to what I represent, my job, my social status?

Am I not a slave to things? In the end, what am I building that is of any value? Where is my personal treasure? Is it in my heart, or elsewhere? May my prayer be a call to God so that he will help me put order in my life. I must always love. I must love first, because to the three key words of the Lourdes message, repeated all along the pilgrimage journey—poverty, prayer, penitence—we must add charity, the love which springs forth from the heart of God.

"Love without measure, devotion without restrictions." May this advice from Bernadette become a lifeline for me so that I will be an artisan of unity every day. Love is the "narrow gate" (Mt 7:13) to the kingdom of heaven where, body and soul, I am invited to enter the house of my true Father, with all who, even without knowing God's name here on earth, will have given their love freely, beyond the rituals and "spoken words."

To have "the vocation" is all too often interpreted only as meaning one entering a religious order; to choose that way of life is really just a consequence of, or an overflowing expression of, the primary singular vocation of all those who are baptized: to love. Bernadette, you wanted to be like everyone else, like Jesus, Mary, and Joseph in Nazareth, clothing yourself with love, having charity as your ideal....

Lord, you place this call from Nazareth into my heart, make it so that I can freely answer it, so that I am not chained to my fears, dreams, escapes, or other "roles I assume." Give me the freedom to say yes. Mary, who is totally free of sin, could say yes and be faithful. To be able to say yes to my vocation, I must be free, and for me to be free, I must be true. Jesus said: "The truth shall set you free." Perhaps it is time for me to make contact again with a priest so I can receive the sacrament of reconciliation, so that I can again find that inner freedom which is so essential to my "fiat," to this "yes," given without any conditions, through which God will lead me where he wants. The humility of my personal recognition as a sinner will open a new road, the one of Love.

Bernadette is a saint, not because she was a religious, but because she loved so much, with a purpose, and with perseverance.... *"My good Mother, give me a heart that is burning for Jesus"* (Personal Diary, 1874).

Bernadette was torn between two choices: the cloister with its "everything for God" and her total dedication to the poor and sick....Her health was against her in both cases. What could unify these two callings, which appear not to be compatible? A union with Christ, *"for the sinners,"* is Bernadette's vocation and is, in fact, my own.

She wrote, *"Love triumphs,"* in her personal diary. Love is another name for penitence because we need a great deal of trust and courage in order to be able to truly love. We must give up our own ideas and will so that we can be silent enough to hear and make others hear, for themselves, the answer to their own questions....Lord, my prayer is a silent cry: give me the strength of love, your strength! *"O Immaculate Mary, O glorious Saint Joseph! And you, Saint John, beloved disciple, give me the great knowledge of how to love! May it be irresistible!..."* (Personal Diary).

REFLECTION QUESTIONS

Am I humble of heart when I pray to God? Am I willing to accept a life of quiet anonymity if that is the will of God? Will I pray for the grace of God to help me overcome my pride, my desire to be recognized and acknowledged for the all the good things that I have done? Can I be satisfied in knowing that it is enough that only God is aware of the good that I do?

The Choice to Love

FOCUS POINT

Immediately he made his disciples get into the boat and go on ahead to the other side, to Bethsaida, while he dismissed the crowd. After saying farewell to them, he went up on the mountain to pray (Mark 6:45–46).

"I came here to hide."

On Wednesday, July 4th, 1866, Bernadette prepared to leave Lourdes. She would be leaving her family and the land she so loved, with its mountains, streams, and trees. And she would also be leaving the grotto, her *"heaven,"* behind. Everyone around her was crying. Her heart was torn apart. She arrived in Nevers on Saturday the 7th, at 10:00 P.M. She was welcomed with joy and curiosity. The next day, she was invited to recount the story of the apparitions for one last time. She told of the eighteen meetings at Massabielle—which occurred from the 11th of February to the 16th of July, 1858—with a lady with blue eyes. From then on, nothing would set her apart from the other religious, except her poor health....

She kept silent about the events at Lourdes, only a few bishops and officials would have the right to question her, in spite of the promise made to her about never having to speak about it again.

She had a difficult novitiate, which was marked by the death of her mother, Louise, on December 8th of the same year. *"The Blessed Virgin wants to make me understand...that she would replace my mother."*

Bernadette confided to Mother Ceyrac: *"I believe that our Lord has not finished testing me because, ever since I have been at Nevers, I have suffered daily in body and soul, but this hasn't stopped me from being content and very happy...."* What an invitation for us to stop listening to ourselves complain! Bernadette consoled her heart by praying beside a statue of the Virgin, located in the garden. The statue was one of Our Lady of the Waters, which reminded her a little of Lourdes. A small votive chapel, dedicated to Saint Joseph, built in 1860, welcomed her like a mysterious and discreet prolongation of the grotto: *"One can pray well in this chapel?—Oh yes! I go there whenever I can."*

Do I, today, have a place where I can go to gather my thoughts and have peace and quiet? Am I waiting for the next pilgrimage, perhaps to Lourdes, as if I have to do a good deed from time to time? Do I have enough faith in the presence of God wherever I am to hear him? Bernadette's story is a story of faithfulness to a rendezvous of prayer—in the garden, close to the statue of Our Lady of the Waters, in the Chapel of St. Joseph, at the Nevers convent. I would also like to take the time to go to a little church, an oratory, or to gaze upon a statue of Mary. There are so many opportunities for prayer. Bernadette showed me, by the way she lived, that we don't have to go to a big church, or to a very holy place, in order to replenish ourselves in God.

If, on the day she took her religious habit, Bernadette said to one of her companions, *"I came here to hide,"* she did so because she was keenly aware that she had been called to live the different aspects of the Lourdes message in Nevers. She did not come to "mortify herself"; she came to die to herself so that she could be reborn in Jesus Christ. One does not have to live in a convent to be able to experience this new birth. I can have it here, today. If someone comes to me and says, "thank you for your silence," it is because I will have allowed another presence to develop between us. Lord, one day, I heard the phrase "thank you for your silence"—me, even though I'm so full of myself and talkative! Ever since then I have understood the fruitfulness of death. One dies to oneself in order to leave room for the Spirit of the Lord, who unites all contradictions.... It is a good way to pray. I presume that Bernadette prayed this same way. I would like Bernadette's silence to change my life!

"I am the broom which the Virgin has used. What do we do with a broom when we finish using it? We put it away, behind the door. That is my place, I am happy there. I will stay there." On the 29th of July, 1866, the little messenger from Lourdes joined the congregation, taking the habit and receiving the name Sister Marie Bernard.

On the 15th of August, she took to her bed. She appeared to be dying on the 25th of October and the bishop received her vows, in haste, in the middle of the night, at the same time as administering the sacrament of anointing of the sick to her. Bernadette quickly recovered and rejoiced at having professed her vows in this manner: *"They can't send me back!"* Life went on in the convent.

One day, in May of 1867, a new arrival—Marie Antoinette Dalais de Lectoure—sought to find the visionary. When they pointed Bernadette out to her, she exclaimed, "That!" Bernadette replied, with a smile: *"Why yes, Miss, it's only that...."* How many times have we encountered people who appear to be insignificant without realizing that they could have an inestimable inner richness? My prayer today will be to pay close attention to whomever I meet. I will think of Bernadette and Mary each time I meet someone who appears unimportant, because now I know that the world's criteria are not God's. Marie Antoinette Dalais de Lectoure described Bernadette to her family in this way: "She seemed very nice, but rather childlike, lively, and spontaneous. There was such a simplicity to her that I would never have had the idea to attribute that role to her." This tells us a great deal about Bernadette's behavior in the convent. She was not playing a role. When she arrived to enter the novitiate, had she not asked, *"Can we skip rope here?"* "Whoever does not receive the kingdom of God as a little child will never enter it" (Lk 18:17).

My Lord, my Father, keep my childlike heart, do not allow the external trappings of "success" force me to play a role to the point that I no longer know who I am: I am your child. Grant me the spontaneity and simplicity which characterize the saints. Open my eyes, Lord, to your true presence in the hearts of the humble, those without title or rank.... Mother Josephine Imbert, the Superior General, said publicly about Bernadette: "She is good for nothing." The bishop had given her "the job of prayer" on October 30th, 1867, when she renewed her religious profession. The job of prayer was given to the one whose choice had been to love because praying is a permanent state for one who loves. They pray by living. They live by praying. May this love-prayer renew my outlook, each of my actions, and my entire being in depth. May my prayer be the golden key to my destiny and my soul.

"Courage, my child, you have found the precious gem that gives access to the kingdom of heaven: love always..." (Mary to Bernadette, meditation in her Personal Diary, 1873).

The members of the congregation of the Sisters of Nevers did not only take the three traditional vows of poverty, chastity, and obedience, they also took a fourth: the vow of charity. This dates back to the congregation's origins, in 1663, and to its founder, Jean Baptist Delaveyne. A child of eleven made this remark to me: "It is the first vow that everyone who consecrates his life to God must take." Bernadette took this vow of charity....This vow of love that is so essential, even if it defies explanation. It would later be suppressed somewhat, after a review of the congregation's constitution. But today, here, now, I can make this "vow of love," like a promise, by uniting myself to Bernadette's prayer. I choose to love— that says it all, and I make it my life's goal. *"I will not live a single moment where I do not love"* (Personal Diary, p. 10).

REFLECTION QUESTIONS

Do I recognize those times in my life when God calls me away from the crowds, the hustle and bustle of daily life, to pray to him in a place of quiet? Am I aware of those moments in the day when I am called to silent reflection, to say a word of thanks or praise, to make a prayer of petition for the welfare of another?

With the Holy Family

FOCUS POINT

The Holy Family is an example of ideal love, an earthly model of the perfect, heavenly love of the Holy Trinity. As a member of the Church, a family that is the people of God, I pray to Saint Joseph, patron of the family, for increased love and devotion towards all of my brothers and sisters, and to accept a humble role of service in this family.

"When we don't know how to pray,
we ask Saint Joseph."

B ernadette is a religious whose weaknesses are gaps by which grace rushes in…. She is perfectly obedient to the rule, above all to (the one of) silence, but with total freedom and great discretion. She cannot understand the Sisters who close their eyes when they must have them open! Her health is a great challenge: *"What could I tell you about myself? I am always a fixture in the infirmary. This time, God held me longer on the cross. Pray a little for me, I need it so much, one must be patient when it lasts so long. So, pray a little for me, so I am granted more patience"* (to Sister Ursule Fardes).

The head of the novices did not understand very well why the Mother of God had chosen someone as simple as Bernadette! In spite of it all, Sister Marie Bernard radiated with a secret joy which shone through in her astonishing gaze, this gaze which struck all who saw her. She already belonged to the mysterious *"next world,"* which Mary had spoken to her about, by suffering greatly in this one. What is this world? It is the world where God became man so that man would become God; the world of the Incarnation that the Lord had definitively entrusted to Joseph: "Joseph, son of David, do not be afraid to take Mary as your wife, for the child conceived in her is from the Holy Spirit" (Mt 1:20).

Bernadette was initiated from within, thanks to her mother Mary, to the true secrets concerning the Holy Family, in this way reuniting the deepest Christian tradition. Teresa of Ávila, a Doctor of the Church, wrote: "If someone can't master prayer, they should call upon the glorious Saint Joseph; they won't run the risk of going astray" (*The Story of Her Life*, chapter VI). It was to Saint Joseph that the Son of God had to unite in order to develop; he was chosen over the brilliant company of the doctors of the Temple....

At the beginning of August, 1872, a year and a half after the death of her beloved father, François, Bernadette spoke these words, which became key words: *"I am going to go see my father..."*—Your father?—*"Don't you know that Saint Joseph is now my father?"*

This invisible presence of Saint Joseph, and assuredly that of Mary, at Bernadette's side, provided her with an astonishing inner strength—by continuing, within her, the workings of this "vitamin for growth" which was the love of her parents during her childhood. And in spite of her health concerns, she was, in fact, the head nurse at the Saint Gildard convent (even if her official title stated that she was only an assistant). In 1872, the house doctor, Robert St. Cyr, wrote: "She was a nurse that performed her duties perfectly. She was small, with a sickly appearance. Her nature was calm and gentle. She cared for the sick with a great deal of intelligence, omitting nothing from the prescribed treatments. She also exuded a great sense of authority and, from me, she received my complete confidence."

Bernadette was not a conceited religious, steeped in piety. She was a responsible woman who was realistic and did not live enclosed in an artificial world. In terms of her spirituality, Bernadette was not ethereal; she was truly living in the realities of this world. You sent yourself to the school of the Holy Family, with Mary as your mother, Joseph as your father, and Jesus as your brother. This is the school I want to go to—the school of the living gospel.

During the war of 1870, after the surrender of Napoleon III, the Saint Gildard convent served as a hospital for wounded soldiers. Bernadette probably took care of some of them. She was afraid of nothing, not even the Prussians: *"God is everywhere, even amongst the Prussians."* "The sickly one" had been transformed into a nurse, who was very close to her "older" sisters. Her own handicap had allowed her to better understand the suffering of others. She didn't only take care of their bodies, but also their hearts; her sharp psychology and good down-home sense were a great help to her companions.

Praying with Bernadette does not consist of a great deal of thinking, but does consist of loving a great deal. Instead of seeking the impossible in my spiritual life, maybe I should "roll up my sleeves" and devote myself to serving others. Lord Jesus, with you, I want to learn to do the simplest things with diligence, perseverance, and with joy. May my work resemble the work in the Nazareth workshop: may it have harmony, creativity, and love for those I serve....

The Holy Trinity is a great mystery to me. My small brain, so swelled and filled with myself, will never understand anything about it. Yet, the family in Nazareth, the earthly projection of the greatest supernatural realities, opens the "narrow gate" (Mt 7:13) to the new world for me.

Bernadette wanted to die saying: "Jesus, Mary, and Joseph." It was the Sisters who surrounded her who would say this invocation, in her stead, at the time of her death. Forget all your previous lofty images of the Holy Family. We are all called to join in the spark of love which unites the members of this first Christian family. Above all, don't do it in a vulgar way, because Christianity is not a statement of ethics or a list of precepts for perfect people. We must not speak of "Christianism"—that is a vile word, an "ism" like a supplementary ideology—we must only attest to our personal adherence to the risen, living Christ. Nothing ages when we are aware of the "today" of God.

No matter what kind of family we have—single parent, divorced and remarried, filled with conflict—we can all be reflections of the Holy Family in as much as we accept the presence of God within us. Perfection is not a Christian "value": our single objective is holiness. The most beautiful flowers grow in manure...as long as we let the gardener do his work!

By recognizing myself to be poor and vulnerable, today, I joyously repeat Mary's words: "Here I am, Lord...let it be with me according to your word" (Lk 1:38). The Holy Family was born out of this offering of love to the love that gives of itself....

Resurrected through my baptism, I know that my mediocrity will become the soil for a new tree where the birds of heaven will make their nests, because I no longer want to live my Christian life like it's a duty, but with enthusiasm—the word signifying "chosen by God"—just like Joseph did, this young man in my world, my contemporary.... He and Mary are inseparable.

REFLECTION QUESTIONS

Is it difficult for me to accept a role of humble service in my Church family? Am I satisfied serving my brothers and sisters in Christ "behind the scenes," without recognition, without fanfare? Am I, like Saint Bernadette, ready to call upon the aid of the Holy Family in my sincere desire "to join in the spark of love which unites the members of this first Christian family"?

DAY FOURTEEN

The Time of the Passion

FOCUS POINT

In the course of suffering, at the time of death, I will keep my eyes squarely on the loving face of my Lord and Savior, Jesus. Because death has been conquered by Jesus Christ, it has been made holy, and is now a transition to eternal happiness in heaven. There is nothing I should fear; the path has been made by Jesus, and I need only follow.

"Pray for me, a poor sinner."

O n the 19th of March, 1879, Father Febvre, the chaplain of the community, asked Bernadette this question: "What particular grace have you asked of Saint Joseph?" She answered: *"I asked him for the grace of a happy death."* Seeing Bernadette's grave tone that was firm and precise, the priest thought that she had a premonition of impending death. She had fallen sick often. On the 3rd of June, 1873, she had received the sacrament of anointing of the sick for the third time. Little by little, she was unable to do any work at Saint Gildard other than the *"work of being sick."*

This was a time when she wrote a great deal in her "Personal Diary," which has already been cited numerous times. It includes a collection of little phrases she recorded or recopied during many retreats. Misery and light paired themselves in these spiritual confidences: *"Don't be afraid to carry the cross naked."* Advice from her confessor, Father Douce, is very evident in these writings. She made certain resolutions and, thus, revealed a little about herself, notably through this poor beggar's prayer to Jesus:

O Jesus, I beg you to give me the bread of humility, the bread of obedience, the bread of charity, the bread of strength in order to break my will and combine it with yours, the bread of inner mortification, the bread of detachment from creatures, the bread of patience so I can withstand the sorrows my heart suffers. O Jesus, you want to crucify me, fiat! The bread of strength to suffer well, the bread of seeing only you in everything always. I want no other friends than Jesus, Mary, and the cross.

Bernadette's final years will show us the steps to the absolute love of Christ, who glorified the Father by dying to wash away the sins of the world.

"My hand trembles like that of an old woman," Bernadette confided to a correspondent in 1876. She was often confined to bed. In September of 1876, Father Douce, the Marist chap-

lain who had been helping her for more than ten years, was replaced by Father Febvre. On September 8, 1877, Father Peyramale died and Bernadette suffered. Her family had disputes which pained her. Also, to better describe Bernadette's cross in Nevers, we must mention the promises which were not kept regarding never having to speak about the apparitions, the dispute between Henri Lasserre (the writer) and Father Sempé (the rector of the burgeoning sanctuary), the illness which prohibited her return to Lourdes for the consecration of the chapel in 1876, and her intolerable pain from the tumor on her knee and her tubercular asthma....

She feared that she had been unfaithful to *"so many graces"*—her final night on earth—to the point of being *"overwhelmed,"* and joined the crucified Christ in her *"white chapel,"* her alcove in the infirmary. From her bed, she participated in the Masses which were being celebrated *"all over the world."* In December of 1877, at the request of Msgr. de Ladoue (Msgr. Forcade's successor as bishop of Nevers), she wrote to Pius IX: *"Holiest of Fathers, what can I do to prove my filial love to you? I can only continue doing what I have been doing up until now, that is to say, suffer and pray."* The pope sent her a little crucifix, with his blessing, which never left her side. When Father Sempé went to question her in 1878, Bernadette had reached the end of her patience and strength.

Finally, she had the holy pictures, which she had pinned to her bed curtains, removed—the one of Saint Bernard, her patron saint, the succentor of Mary—keeping only her crucifix. She said: *"That one is enough for me."*

On the 28th of March, 1879, she received the sacrament of anointing of the sick for the fourth time.... On the 15th of April, she confided the following to Sister Nathalie, who came to visit her: *"I am afraid...I have received so many graces and I have profited so little from them!"*

The following day, the 16th of April, she extended her arms like a cross and cried out, *"My God!"* She seemed to have fallen prey to terrible torture. Dying, Bernadette twice repeated, *"Holy Mary, Mother of God, pray for me, a poor sinner!"* After having asked for something to drink, like Christ on the cross, she gently fell asleep and died....

Her body, still incorrupt after three exhumations, lies in a glass reliquary at the Saint Gildard convent.

The daughter of the miller from Boly, had whispered, during her passion: *"I have been ground in the mill like a grain of wheat."* During Holy Week, just before her death, she had said: *"The passion touches me more when I read it than when someone explains it to me...."*

What comment do we have the right to make when we are faced with such an imitation of Jesus Christ? Let us pray in silence. With Bernadette, I read about the death of the Lord. And I think about my friend Jack, a family man, suffering from cancer, who asked me to accompany him so he could bathe himself in the pools at Lourdes in the middle of winter. Before diving into the waters of the spring, he had embraced the small statue of Mary that an orderly had handed to him, saying in a lowered voice (and not realizing I could hear him): "Mother, I do not ask you for physical healing, but for the inner strength to unite myself to the suffering of your Son." I cried like a baby and he radiated with serenity and joy. What Bernadette had lived through was not a heroic episode of a past era, reserved for the elite class of canonized saints. During each little daily crisis, a gesture of love can also unite me with the crucified Jesus. I don't have much courage, I even panic—I must recognize that—at the thought of suffering. I hope that I will not be asked to live the passion of Bernadette, or of my friend Jack, but the little death of each moment that can equally bring rebirth and meaning. That is where we find the miracle which truly heals the world of its faults: *"Not consolation, but strength and patience,"* like Bernadette said in the last moments of her earthly life.

This is incomprehensible, unacceptable, and unbearable from a human viewpoint. Love never follows any rules: don't look for any explanation, except through the ultimate love for Jesus. The secret that Bernadette shares with me today is: *"Jesus is my only Goal, Jesus is my only Master, Jesus is my only Model, Jesus is my only Joy, Jesus is my only Treasure, Jesus is my only Friend!"* I am agonizingly sick with sin and in danger. I can pray with Bernadette who said: *"I can't say any long prayers. I beg by praying in spurts."* What that means is praying in short prayers like cries of love: *"My God, I offer this to you. My God, I love you! My God, I believe in you, I hope in you...."*

Bernadette began her Hail Mary, which she couldn't finish....

Two big tears ran down her cheeks as she was still holding the crucifix on her heart while she was dying. Her funeral, on the 19th of April, will have been almost like a celebration, by evoking the hidden splendor of her soul: the Lord lifts up the humble.

On the 30th of May, they would bury the little body of Sister Marie Bernard in the St. Joseph Chapel, where it would remain for almost fifty years....

Did the Blessed Virgin tell her that she would die young? Bernadette had written: *"I will do everything for heaven.... There, I will find my Mother in the brilliance of her glory."*

Eternal life has already begun for me. These few years on

earth are a starting point for the next world. Lord, make it so that I don't miss this launching point, that I don't waste the precious time which has been given to me so I can love. Everything goes by so quickly…I don't want to lose a single moment.

Throughout our passions, conflicts, and the red roses of our feelings, a metamorphosis is occurring which could be symbolized by the yellow roses placed on Mary's feet—they were the color of gold purified by fire. A yellow rose, the symbol of the flesh which was transfigured in the light of the Resurrected One….

REFLECTION QUESTIONS

Do I allow a period of suffering in my life to serve as a means to deepen my faith in God? Am I able to unite my pain in suffering with the passion of Jesus, and increase my understanding of his great love for me when he died for my sins? Am I able to ask God for the grace of patience in the midst of enduring suffering and chronic pain?

A Happy Death:
The Death of One's Self

FOCUS POINT

There is God's will and there is my will. My only desire is to join my will with his, to live a life of service to God's will—there can be no greater joy. My desires—seeking those things that are less than God but serving them as if they were—must be abandoned in favor of God's plan for me. All I need do is pray, and it will be given to me. "Ask, and it will be given you; search, and you will find;...For everyone who asks receives" (Mt 7:7–8).

"If you knew what I saw down there....If you knew how good the Blessed Virgin is....

We must pray a great deal for sinners. It is a recommendation from the Blessed Virgin."

B ernadette had left Lourdes, her family, and her beloved grotto on a Wednesday. It was on Wednesday, March 19th, that she put her own death into the hands of Saint Joseph: she died, a month later, on the most beautiful Wednesday in 1879, Easter Wednesday. She had expressed the desire to die while she was saying, *"Jesus, Mary, Joseph,"* the traditional invocation, which is a concise description of the world that she lived in, more and more. In her Personal Diary, she had explained that the passion of the Lord and his humble life in Nazareth were the two places of *"pure love."* His death had harmonized the two opposing poles of his life. On Easter Sunday, she had said: *"My passion will last until I die."* She lived this passion in the simplicity of Nazareth but with a terrible intensity, through suffering and patience, which greatly affected those who witnessed it. *"Through love for Jesus, I should be victorious over myself or die"* (Personal Diary). Bernadette's very last prayer had been a recitation of the Hail Mary, which she said very slowly. Twice, she repeated the phrase, *"pray for me...poor sinner...poor sinner."* This was an expression which was part of the prayers for the dead included in the congregation's manual, and surely took on particular meaning when it came out of Bernadette's mouth.

When I ask Mary to pray for us "at the hour of our death," it refers to the death of my self. May Mary teach me to let the presence live within me of this Other, from whom I have received everything—life, progress, my very self. He is my true identity: "Jesus is the Other!" Mary, the Immaculate Conception, made me understand this. God uses every way possible—all the way to becoming flesh—so that he can nourish and regenerate me because he wants me to make myself resemble him and to call me by my name: Immaculate.

Mary is the masterpiece, created out of God's love. She

wanted to resemble Bernadette so that Bernadette could resemble her: she adopted her same height, her youth, even her
native patois. *"Your heart and mine together will become
one and only one heart"* (Mary to Bernadette, meditation,
Personal Diary). Bernadette learned to have grace, she repeated
messages from heaven and prayed for sinners. This aspect of
Bernadette's prayer is fundamental and it brings her into the
celestial psychology, turned entirely toward unassuming love:
"The Son of Man came not to be served but to serve" (Mt
20:28).

If she prayed for herself, it was because she was a sinner,
and these would be her very last earthly words. She prayed
and suffered for the sinners: her life, her sufferings, belong to
them as they also do to the souls in purgatory (which she
often thought about). But these latter souls were assured of
their salvation, whereas the sinners were on the brink of the
abyss: *"We never do enough for the conversion of sinners."*
She did exactly what Jesus did by living and dying for us,
with complete interior poverty, keeping nothing for himself.

To better understand the radial novelty of this aspect, we
must listen to Jesus speaking to the young Marcel Van, who
died on July 10th, 1959, under admirable conditions, and
whose cause for beatification has been introduced: "You must
never work to gain merits with the intention of keeping them
so that you can gain eternal happiness. If you have such an
intention, it is absolutely a certainty that the kingdom of
heaven will not be yours" (*Love Knows Me*, spiritual writings by Marcel Van, Le Sarment Fayard, 1990, p. 196).

Bernadette, to whom nothing belonged, lived this divine
truth. What road of purification I must still have to travel!
The road is long but the light shines at the end of my night:
God wants me to be a saint and, above all, he wants me to be

his, totally his, like Jesus gave himself up to the arms of his Father in the great silence of the cross.

There is another original aspect of Bernadette's prayer, which connects her to Teresa of Ávila, the first woman Doctor of the Church: she knew through Mary, that Joseph, her Father, was "the patron saint of a happy death." Let us meditate on Teresa of Ávila's words from chapter XXXII of *The Story of Her Life*:

> One day, after Communion, the Lord asked me to work, with all my strength, to establish a new convent. He promised to help me and assured me that he would be well served there. I was to name it St. Joseph. He would hold one door, our Lady would hold the other, and Christ would be in the middle....

Jesus, who is present in our midst when we are gathered together in his name—when we love each other—learned to pray while he worked with Saint Joseph. A happy death is, therefore, the death of one's self. That is the heart of evangelical teaching. Therefore, let us live this experience as often as possible, by receiving, like a gift, simplicity, modesty, and perseverance. No human work can bring us that. The following are the most moving lines from Bernadette's diary, written in an exhausted, almost totally spent, hand: *"The means that God puts at our disposal: the light, that is to say, our rules."* Today, I translate this to mean the gospel. *"As for us, we must show good will, that is to say, energetic, courageous, steadfast, perseverant."* The greatest temptation is to get discouraged—reject it.

And when, finally, we are again faced with our radical poverty, because we don't know how to pray, let the Holy

Spirit sigh within us, like the apostle Paul said to the Romans (8:26–27): "The Spirit helps us in our weakness; for we do not know how to pray as we ought, but that very Spirit intercedes with sighs too deep for words. And God, who searches the heart, knows what is the mind of the Spirit, because the Spirit intercedes for the saints according to the will of God."

During these hours of prayer, we have left the temple, the cavern of thieves, by dying to all appearances, so that we can go meet Jesus in silence, where worldly reality has no meaning. The Holy Spirit will become like the air we breathe. Life is different, *"given over to Joseph and Mary,"* according to Sister Marie Bernard Soubirous (Letter to her brother, Pierre, November 3, 1876).

REFLECTION QUESTIONS

Do I seek to abandon my selfish desires in favor of God's will? Am I able to pray that God's will be done in my life, despite the suffering that might occur? Am I excited about the joy of a deepened relationship with God that will result from my submission to his will?

Evaluation Questions

USE THESE QUESTIONS to evaluate your fifteen days with Bernadette of Lourdes: What happened to me during these days? What struck me as important? What did I feel about what I read? What was my mood? Did I notice any changes in my mood? What did the Lord show me? Was any particular spiritual path revealed to me? Are there any points that I might need to return to for more reflection and prayer? What do I most want to remember? Do I feel the need to make any resolution or commitment as the result of these days of prayer?

———

We have come to the end of our fifteen days together which have introduced us into the *"next world."* Like a seed that has taken root, let us say the prayer of the students at the Gospel School in Lourdes and the Our Lady of the Dawn community (written by Father André Cabes):

> Blessed are you, God, our Father, to have created Mary so beautiful and for having given her to us as our Mother at the foot of Jesus' cross. Blessed are you for having called us, like Bernadette, to see Mary in your light and to drink from the wellspring of your heart.

Mary, you know the poverty and the sins in our lives and the lives of the world. We want to entrust ourselves to you, today, totally and without reservation. Through you, we will be reborn every day through the power of the Holy Spirit. We will live the life of Jesus, serving our brothers. Mary, teach us to carry the life of the Lord within ourselves. Teach us the yes in your heart.

Lourdes, October 7, 1997,
the feast day of Our Lady of the Rosary

Further Reading About the Message of Lourdes

Bertrin, G. *Lourdes: A History of Its Apparitions and Cures.* Gordon Press, 1973.

Brown, Wilmott G. *The Significance of Lourdes, Fátima, and Medjugorje As Explained in Scripture.* W. G. Brown, 1995.

Cranston, Ruth. *Miracle of Lourdes.* Doubleday, 1988.

Grosso, Stephen. *Experiencing Lourdes: An Intimate View of the Miraculous Shrine and Its Pilgrims.* Servant, 1996.

Laurentin, René. *Bernadette of Lourdes.* Minneapolis: Winston Press, 1979.

Lovasik, Lawrence G. *Our Lady of Lourdes.* Catholic Book Publishing, 1985.

Pouvillon, Emile. *Bernadette.* BVD Publishing, 1996.

Trochu, Francis. *St. Bernadette Soubirous.* TAN Books Publications, 1985.

Urbide, Fernando and Engler, Dan. *Bernadette: The Princess of Lourdes.* CCC of America, 1990.